BOOK 1: RISE OF THE MOTHER

# SAVING THE WORLD ONE BOOB AT A TIME

*Shona Reidy*

Copyright © 2024 by Shona Reidy

All rights reserved. No part of this publication may be reproduced, distributed, or transmitted in any form or by any means, including photocopying, recording, or other electronic or mechanical methods, without the prior written permission of the publisher, except in the case of brief quotations embodied in critical reviews and certain other noncommercial uses permitted by copyright law.

Book Design by HMDpublishing

ISBN: 978-0-6456805-2-2

Instagram Handle: @savingtheworldoneboobatatime

Disclaimer: This book is based on true events however all names have been changed to protect the identity of all people for personal and legal reasons, the author maintains that any character's resemblance to real, living persons is just a coincidence.

*For my babies, Thankyou for choosing me to be your mummy.
Xxx*

# CONTENTS

INTRODUCTION . . . . . . . . . . . . . . . . . . . . . . . . . . 6

CHAPTER 1.
*MY OWN RISE AS A MOTHER: MIND, BODY, AND MILK* . . . . . . . . . . . . . . . . . . . . . . . . 11

CHAPTER 2.
*RISE MOTHER RISE (LISTEN TO YOUR BABY & BREASTFEEDING GUIDE)* . . . . . . 53

CHAPTER 3.
*THE MINDFUL MOTHER (BREASTFEEDING MEDITATIONS)* . . . . . . . . . . . . 81

CHAPTER 4.
*PREPARING FOR YOUR RISE (SOUL WORK FOR MOTHERS AND PARTNERS)* . . . . . . . 91

CHAPTER 5.
*CONTINUE TO RISE* . . . . . . . . . . . . . . . . . . . . . 122

CHAPTER 6.
*GO FORTH AND CONQUER* . . . . . . . . . . . . . . . 133

RESOURCES TO RISE . . . . . . . . . . . . . . . . . . . . . 138
MEDITATIONS . . . . . . . . . . . . . . . . . . . . . . . . . . 139
ABOUT THE AUTHOR . . . . . . . . . . . . . . . . . . . . 140

~

*This book is for mothers, both new and "wise."
For the women who are procreating and understand the need to cherish the process.
For the women that know that the journey is the true joy, and that there is no final destination with motherhood.
For the women that split their hearts open daily for the little people in their lives.
For the women that know, in their deepest heart of hearts, that being a mother is of such importance that they simply must get it right.
For the mothers that need reassurance that anxiety & fear in motherhood is "love on light speed" – it is your instinct, dear mother, not a mental health condition.
This book is dedicated to women who can feel that inner wolf inside of them, howling to be given permission to listen to the churning in her stomach. To be reassured that that churning of fear and anxiety is just your instincts turning on, and that fear is your way of protecting your child.
Growl, and growl LOUD.
For the mothers that wanted to breastfeed but, for physical or emotional reasons, couldn't, I see you and I hear you – you can still feel the Rise of the Mother without breastfeeding.
This book is also for the mother that cannot or will not breastfeed,
I love you and have counselled you, too.
This book is for women (and their partners), to give them the opportunity to RISE as mothers.
God Bless you, mothers. You are walking the most incredible path a human being has the honour to walk.*

*Love, Shona xoxo*

# INTRODUCTION

*The number one reason breastfeeding doesn't work is stress.*

*The number one solution for stress is meditation.*

One day, at some point between my separation and divorce, I was vacuuming the house and the epiphany hit me, like a lightning bolt inside my searching mind.

I stopped vacuuming and looked up, "Good one, God!" I exclaimed. "You're SO right, this will really help mums to breastfeed!"

In between juggling my new roles as mother and breadwinner, I was trying to find a way to help the mothers that I counselled to lengthen their breastfeeding journey by overcoming the number one reason they usually couldn't continue: stress.

I myself was an avid meditator, and it seemed only natural at that time to come up with breastfeeding meditations and workshops, which I truly hoped would help mothers and their partners better serve their children.

*My parenting philosophy*

I have found that parents struggle to be the parents THEY want to be, not some cookie-cutter forms of their family heritage, which might or might not serve them or their child.

I believe children *do* come with a manual, and we access that manual simply by watching, listening to, and respecting them, as the new souls they are when they come into your life.

So many times, I hear people give this advice to new parents: "Make the baby fit into *your* life – don't change your life for the baby." I think that is the most dysfunctional advice I've *ever* heard in my time as a mother. How on *Earth* will that raise an emotionally intelligent, secure, and self-assured human being? Applying that strategy tells me that you are wanting to push your own agenda and ideals onto a new soul, disallowing it the opportunity to blossom into the brilliant human of free will that God meant them to be.

I have always felt it a great honour to be a mother, and I don't take that responsibility lightly, which is why I have always stopped and listened to my children. Respecting their decisions (countless wishes for sugar obviously aside) I've discovered it natural to create happy, resilient and very much independent, "free to be themselves" children.

I call it "mindful and faithful" parenting, and it is definitely the easiest way towards a self-sovereign journey for you and your child. It's an ever-present experience that helps you to marvel on a daily basis at the beauty of parenthood. The journey itself becomes the joy, and the memories are simply testimonies to the respect you paid you and your child for honouring each and every moment. Both your moments and theirs.

My God-given idea on how meditations help you to breastfeed and parent are, in my opinion, the most brilliant of all of our mental health creations. To better oneself, it's important to begin to be the master of your mind. One of the greatest teachings I've heard is that I can choose my thoughts; I don't have to think about whatever falls into my mind, especially from an external source that may be stressful to me (such as someone else's opinion about the way I am mothering). As **Proverbs 23:7 says, "s he [a man] thinks in his heart, so is he."**

**You can see it like this:** *Where the mind goes, the energy flows.*

God is concerned about the hidden man of the heart, which is our inner life – and our inner life is what we think about. And like the scripture above says, the way we think determines how we live and who we are. That's why we need to think about what we're thinking about.

How does this work with breastfeeding, then? Through teaching your mind to tell you to overcome the hurdles that stand in the way of you being able to breastfeed (stress), you will invariably overcome them With the right mind-tools at hand (such as guided meditations), it will truly become that simple.

The element of breastfeeding that ensures success is the hormone oxytocin. This beautiful hormone is the love hormone, and without it being elicited/triggered, the milk cannot be released from the breast. When you are stressed, your milk will not release from the breast, and eventually this will cease your breastfeeding journey. However, the best way to overcome stress is with a relaxing meditation, which uses the power of your mind.

The meditations I share with you in this book I have used on myself as a breastfeeder and then on many, many others, for the most AMAZING and natural results I've seen to continue your breastfeeding relationship. (found on pages 56-63).

*Breastfeeding: How it all works*

We need to stimulate the hormone oxytocin so that the milk is "ejected" (i.e., let down from the breast). Stress inhibits this hormone, so if you are not stressed, then you will be able to have a let down.

My meditations will train your mind and body to get that let down to work in the middle of the night, without needing to get up and open a packet of biscuits or take a pill. Instead, you can just repeat the meditations I teach you and a let down will occur.

The mind is a powerful tool, and we as human beings are made so perfectly. God gave you the power of self-control, so use that control for your breastfeeding journey in the most natural way possible, with meditation and the knowledge that with the right support tools, you can 100% breastfeed. This information is even applicable to those that have Insufficient Glandular Tissue (IGA), this is where your breasts don't have sufficient glands to produce enough milk for a standard feed, and only applies to 2% of Mothers. These meditations will help you relax too. Though you still may need to have mixed feed, you will be more empowered and have a more enjoyable experience. By utilising the beautiful meditations I have been gifted from the Great Inspiration Above, I hereby present this book to you, I begin with my own rise, this is to show you the adversities I have personally overcome, and continue to overcome, to be the best Mother I can possibly be.

The meditations and skills you need to enter into your new role as Mother (and Father) are shared after my own story. I pray you enjoy the journey to self, and dedicate yourself to the Rise of becoming the Mother (and Father) you choose to be.

# Chapter 1.

## MY OWN RISE AS A MOTHER: MIND, BODY, AND MILK

I need to tell you about this one time, when I nearly lost my mind.

If you yourself are sitting on the edge of life, then perhaps this story will help you come back, and realise you're not the only one out there.

It's not until you lose your mind, that you realise how much of it you had in the first place, nor how strong it can be, when you rebuild it, brick by brick – or really, neurone by neurone.

It's not until you lose your mind so completely and utterly that you question whether your head is still on your neck, and whether you will ever be capable of thinking a rational thought again. When you lose your mind, you lose your connection with yourself, your soul, you lose everything.

The colour in the world GOES AWAY.

The bars of mental prisons become debilitating blocks inside your mind.

The anxiety, for me was like a cloak around my head that had heavy metal chains attached to the front, like huge iron drawstrings that swung down past my face, dragging bricks either side of me.

Every day of my mental breakdown was a torment I wouldn't wish on *anybody*.

I thought that pushing a baby out of my body made me strong; I thought having my nipples torn to shreds in the pursuit to feed my baby made me tough.

No, no, and no.

Let's back up a little bit. In June 2014, during a pre-nursing placement I get a flu shot.

Two weeks later, I woke up the in the shower, naked, wet, and pregnant, and with NO IDEA how long I had been there.

I had no idea what time of day it was, or even how many weeks pregnant I was.

reached up and touched my hair: soapy? Slimy? Conditioned?

*It's still dry*, I think as calmly as possible.

OK, so my hair is still dry, so I must have just hopped in the shower.

Next, I think about my three-year-old daughter. *Oh God, where is she?*

"Emily?" I call out to her but hear nothing in return. Instead, I feel the rush of blood to my heart, the muscles tightening. I'm determined not to panic – *I am fine, I am fine, I am FINE...*

"EMILLYYYYY!" I call out, with a tremble in my voice. No response.

And then I release all of my anxiety: "EMMMMILLLLLLYYYYY!"

I feel sick and I turn off the shower – *I need to find my daughter.*

As I proceed to walk through the house naked, I silently note my pregnancy and wonder when I got pregnant.

In the kitchen, I still haven't found my daughter, but I'm distracted by the kettle – should I make myself a cup of tea? Isn't that what they do in the movies, have a cuppa and sit down?

I flick the kettle on and search the kitchen for a newspaper. When I hear the kettle boil, I remember to get a spoon out. *One sugar*, I mutter to myself, *one sugar, one sugar...*

I find myself looking in the drawer, and I see sharp steak knives.

My pregnant stomach, resting in front of the steak knives. I wonder, fleetingly of course, if I should cut my stomach off, but I feel a knee-jerk reaction of fear and slam the drawer shut: *What the hell?!*

Back in the moment, I resume the hunt for my daughter. scream for her, rushing to cover my nudity, realising I'm losing my mind and wondering why I'm showing signs of PND, nearly four months antenatally.

Eventually find her, in her bedroom playing with her dolls. She couldn't hear me, she said, and was alarmed that I was nude, red-faced and a bit cross with her.

I fall to my knees in front of her and just cuddle her. As I'm hugging her, decide NOT to say anything to the Father (Frank). If I do, I see padded cells and hospital beds looming in my future. So, despite my terror, I write it off as a panic attack and pray it doesn't happen again.

But It does. And it gets worse, much, *much* worse.

*Dark thoughts*

The alarming thoughts begin to take shape daily: fleeting thoughts of bizarre, macabre and tragic thoughts of murder and horror.

I'll pass a battery drill....and wonder, *how would that feel going into my stomach? How would that look going through someone's head, or my own head?*

I shake off the thoughts and grit my teeth, determining that they are just "fleeting thoughts" – of course I'm not going to *do* those things…

But I start to lay awake at night, wondering if the battery drill was put away, but too scared to check in case I were to pick it up, too scared to ask in case would be forced to admit why I was asking. Too scared to breathe.

Exhaustion was very quick to settle in, and being pregnant, hormonal, and mentally depraved, my insanity was deepening.

I would often set my daughter up in front of the telly, making sure she was fed and dressed, and then go into the kitchen walk in circles, muttering to myself in my own madness. I walked in front of the oven, turned left at the dishwasher, then left at the pantry, walked in front of the oven, turned left at the dishwasher, then again at the pantry…

I felt like I could contain myself there. Somehow, it helped me contain the madness that was enveloping me.

I finally received a glimmer of hope, while attending a friend's wedding.

Despite the cries of "you're glowing!", I felt like crap and just wished I was in bed. But a blast from the past in the form of a bubbly blonde friend saved my life.

Ladies, oversharing is a gift, and talking about your "stuff" may just save someone's life, like it did for me.

My friend Sarah bubbled up next to me, drunk and enjoying time with my daughter. She sees I'm pregnant and, noticing I'm a bit low, she proceeds to tell me how she got "antenatal depression" whilst pregnant with her twins.

I had originally been unamused at her "happy arrival" at my table, but she has my full attention now.

"You had what?" I lean in, needing to hear *everything*, and knowing deeply that this may be what is wrong with me.

She explains that she had alarming thoughts and would sit on the couch for hours at a time, unable to move or to talk to people. She would be zoned out and had no appetite, and she had felt profoundly depressed, though

Tick, tick, and multiple ticks – she was explaining my current life!

"So, what happened?" I asked her.

"Oh, they medicated the heck out of me," she chirped happily. "And I had the twins and they are fine and I'm fine and it's all just fine now!"

She buzzed off to dance with my daughter, and all of a sudden, I didn't feel so shit. I felt a veil of understanding descend over me, like magic snow. And just like the snow that woke up the Scarecrow, the Cowardly Lion, and Dorothy, this wakes me up too, and I start to feel. Hope.

## *A diagnosis*

I say nothing to Frank until the following Tuesday, as we are driving o the hospital for a midwife appointment. Unbeknownst to him, I have rung ahead with my concerns for my mental health, and they are "ready and waiting" for me. In the meanwhile, I need to let him in on the secret.

"Um...I think there's something wrong with me."

He looks at me and says nothing. Then he looks at me again and says, "Don't be silly."

I try again: "No, I really think that there's something wrong with me. I mean, not wrong with *me*, I mean. Something wrong with my mind. I think I've gone mental or something."

*Winning*, I think to myself as I wait for him to respond. I mean, I am going insane after all! Then I giggle internally at my looniness.

When he does respond, his tone of voice indicates that a fight is looming. We don't do pregnant and babies very well as a couple, unfortunately; the happier days have been left behind us in the nightclubs, and tension is our middle name. But I take a deep breath and launch into it, spewing it all out in a torrent of information.

He stops and looks at me. "There's nothing wrong with you; you're just pregnant!"

I pause, take another deep breath, and launch again: "I haven't told you a lot about what has been going on in my mind, because I didn't want you to worry, but now I know what is sort of going on, and the midwife said its OK and that I won't need to go into a padded cell, that everything is going to be ok."

He looks appropriately confused, and I continue to talk, despite the fear and anxiety tearing at my chest. I tell him *everything*. By the time we get to hospital, he is now appropriately worried, as well, and I'm starting to shit myself: *what the midwife was lying and there* is *a padded cell?*

But we meet with the midwife and go over the usual pregnancy stuff. But then she asks how I'm feeling about the "alarming thoughts."

I see Frank look at her with shock, as if he was hoping everything I said in the car was a joke.

"Frightened," I reply, "and I've only just had the courage to tell Dad here, so he's a bit in shock, I think." I look over at him and his face is deadpan. I know him well, and this face is serious – now he's concerned that all that he's been told really might be happening to me ,and I panic again: *crap, will he be mad at me?*

"OK," she replies quickly. "I've got you booked in with the perinatal psych nurses. They will see you this afternoon...in fact, if you head down there now, we will be able to get you in a little earlier – would that be ok?"

I nod: *yes, please*.

He looks stunned. *Shit*, I think again, *am I in trouble for this?* I immediately feel guilt for "getting sick," and I feel like I've failed him as a wife.

When we meet with a psych nurse, I explain everything to her. As I give her the blow by blow on my alarming thoughts, Frank watches her.

She reacts calmly.

"It's antenatal depression," she calmly tells us. She turns to my husband and says, "There's nothing wrong with your wife."

I see him relax, finally reaching over to hold my and comfort me. "So, she's going to be OK?"

"Oh yes," responds, and I cry with relief. "We will just get her to her doctor and medicate her – it's perfectly safe – and we will just monitor her throughout the pregnancy. Once she has the baby, its going to be OK."

I breathe out a sigh of relief and say, "So that's what I have, antenatal depression?"

"Yes", she responds, "You have antenatal depression and you're going to be OK."

So, there *is* a name for it. *This is a real thing.*

Never in my life have I been so relieved by a diagnosis. Having answers to what is going on is a huge fucking relief. No padded cell for me.

After the diagnosis, we went to get the amniotic fluid test done, but the nurse took one look at me and said, "NO. I don't want to risk this – you might lose the baby. It's a millimetre chance I could basically fuck this up and you'll lose the baby."

Well, she didn't say it *exactly* like that, but it's definitely how it sounded to my very anxious ears. She took an ultrasound, though, and plain as the nose on your face was that little doodle floating between his legs. I was so excited to find out the sex of my unborn baby. I don't know why, but it was the absolute highlight of my pregnancy, knowing I was having my son.

*More darkness before the dawn*

But then you guessed it, things got WORSE. I genuinely don't know how or why, but they just did. I think the decline was so great that by the time I had alerted the authorities (so to speak), I was far worse than we had realised.

I had to wait to get into the doctor for a few days (which felt like years), and then I had to wait for hours (again, feeling like years) to see her. Then I had to go through the rigmarole of her potentially not wanting to medicate me unless she saw the referral from the psych nurse, and of course I didn't bloody well have that on me, so I was a shaking bundle of nerves; a right mess.

I did finally get the meds, though unfortunately they were not an overnight fix.

"Four to six weeks", said the doctor, "before they are 100% effective. Even then, they may not be, and we may need to up your dose which I am hesitant to do, because as you can read, they might cause respiratory or heart complications in your unborn child."

You know, all the information a mad pregnant woman needs from a doctor (who clearly has no bedside manner).

*And by then I'll have killed the whole town with a battery drill*, I think to myself. *Bloody hell.*

So, I trudged through mud daily during this pregnancy, all whilst working part-time and then doing my nursing placement, mothering (unsuccessfully) a three-year-old, renovating a new home, and attempting to be a loving nurturing wife and cook bloody dinner.

The next four to six weeks were a huge battle for me and my failing brain. Zoning out was a daily, if not twice daily, occurrence. I would drive with my lunchbox on the seat beside me so that I could tell if it was full or empty, thus knowing instantly whether I was going to or from work.

Daycare would ring me ten minutes after drop-off to let me know my child was safe and happy…but mainly so I would know where she was.

Showers were either not taken due to too many zone outs, or taken quickly, and hair unwashed, as that took too long. So, on top of feeling crazy, I didn't smell the best and I was getting fatter and frumpier by the day.

Plus, my relationship with my daughter was teetering on non-existent. I could barely speak to her, and I'd sit on the couch praying she wouldn't speak to me. When she did, I'd start to rock (yes, as in the fetal position rock you see in the movies) and put on the TV and let her eat whatever she wanted to, just so she wouldn't talk to me, because I couldn't handle letting her down.

And if she had a tantrum, which three-year-olds do, I would be on my knees crying in front of her, begging her to stop crying because Mummy is sick and can't handle it. She was often shocked out of her tantrums due to my dramatic behaviour. I'd then spend every bedtime reading her multiple books to make up for the shittiness of the day and weeping whilst apologising to her for being so sick.

I was burdening those little shoulders with so much! The mum guilt was tearing my chest apart every day due to the aftermath of this bloody anxiety storm.

However, six weeks (the longest six weeks of my bloody life, I assure you) into the meds being taken, they kicked in like a racehorse on the home straight, and I "woke up" feeling like I was "normal" again overnight.

I could get to sleep without worrying I was going to kill everyone, and I could start to play with my daughter again.

I was able to wash myself properly, dress in clothes that made me feel almost pretty, put on make up, and I even started cooking nutritious food again.

In fact, it was this episode that reminded me of the gut-brain link and had me swearing to *never* let myself get sick again and to *always* put my health first so that I was capable of looking after my family.

After my beautiful boy was born, my mental state didn't decline any further; in fact, I was happier than ever, and the horror that had occurred mid-pregnancy seemed a lifetime ago. The psych nurses checked in on me only twice post birth and said I was fine and that they were confident I was to have a "nice life." And I intended to do so.

For the years after this incredibly disturbing experience though, I still got disorientated. For example, I would be watching the news and it might show a suburb I knew really well, such as a previous hometown. But for the life of me, I couldn't think where it was. I couldn't picture how to get there; I couldn't orientate myself in the street, even though I knew I could recognise it. It would take seconds, sometimes minutes, before I could get myself there and picture it clearly in my head.

So, for many years, I honestly felt like something was "broken." Once I got off the medications a year later, and started treating my brain with more respect than ever before, I started to feel amazing, in control and certain nothing will happen like that again. But if it does, I'm OK with that, because my bounce back is INCREDIBLE, as I've been shown.

*Finding Mind*

So, once you lose something, how do you find it again? This is especially confusing when "it" is still physically there, just not functioning properly.

I will never forget that split second, whilst standing in my bedroom, heavily pregnant, and waiting for the medications to kick in, feeling like I was out of control to the point whereby I might, just might, be capable of doing something horrible. I thought, *Oh bother, I've lost my mind*. And when I surrendered to that, it let the insanity unravel deeper and deeper around my existence, like taking a bad trip and wondering if you'll ever get out of it.

When you lose your mind, you lose everything that goes along with it: intelligence to make decisions. Confidence in your ability to do *anything*. Thought processes are halted and almost cease to exist for a period of time. New neurons are not being created due to the halt in activity, so surely brain decay has begun.

When I was studying my nursing degree, I remember watching a clip-on dementia prevention. A couple in Australia, who were diagnosed in their 30s with early-onset dementia, were using study to combat the disease. The brain, they explained, is just like a muscle: if you don't use it, it will atrophy (shrink). But if you do use it, it will flex and grow. This, they claimed, was staving off the dementia. Fiendishly disciplined, they spent hours and hours every day reading new information, studying, and constantly learning new things, languages, skills.

After my mental breakdown, I remembered this, and decided that I needed to do the same – rebuild my brain, brick by brick.

*What better way to rebuild it*, I thought, *than studying for my diploma in counselling?*

So, when my son was only a few months old, I got to work on rebuilding my brain, by learning about how the brain works. This proved to be exactly what I needed, and re-commencing my nursing studies after my break was also fuel for the brain fire. I started to feel better after every study session.

As a schoolgirl, I liked homework, but since discovering my purpose as a breastfeeding counsellor in 2011, I have loved pouring my heart and soul into learning. I now seek it daily; it's so completely necessary for me to be doing "something" new every day, even if its listening to a new song, or saying a new word. My brain is my best friend now and it responds really well when I'm paying attention to it!

I also started using meditation to start setting my brain on a new path, and I knew that I needed to do it daily. But getting up early to do so was proving to be difficult. My son was a wakeful baby and my daughter was too, needing me to feed her every two hours until she was two-and-a-half years old. (For those critics out there, these are all normal behaviours – denying a child milk and comfort is incredibly *dangerous* for milk supply and for the baby's emotional wellbeing. Not to mention disruptive of the innate flow of love and bonding a mother and child need to develop on their *own time*, not someone else's.)

By this stage I was like a Secret Services Mother, and my mental capacity for sleep deprivation was fine-tuned. Don't sleep? Sure, I can do that!

However, my son has a MTHFR gene mutation I wasn't aware of at the time, and with the immunisation schedule so heavy in the first year of his life, he was hospitalised twice and waking every 45 minutes nightly so that I could feed him, nourishing and flushing out the toxins his little body was unable to eliminate naturally.

After a year of being woken this frequently, however, my body was starting to fade away. I had also started to enjoy wine a little too frequently. After the fright from the year before, we had decided to try to relax and enjoy life more, but my wine habit was interfering with my health, and I was alarmed to find myself so darn tired that I was even thinking I needed to potentially wean my son at eleven months old. Which went against every value and belief I had as a breastfeeding Mother, I was determined to feed him to two years of age.

By the time my son was 12 months old, I was a third of the way through my counselling diploma, but I was growing fatigued by his constant waking.

As a breastfeeding counsellor, it was very important to me to feed him until the age of two because the World Health Organisation (WHO) recommends this. Plus I fed my daughter until three, so it was scary for me to think of weaning at less than a year. But I was struggling so much to get going every day, and my solution of having a little "tipple" every night was just making me go backwards. Plus, I have the same MTHFR gene mutation as my son, which was undiagnosed at the time as well. My body isn't designed to drink alcohol, the inability to detoxify was throwing my health into a fast downward spiral.

*The Magic Beans*

I began looking at my nutrition. Since being introduced to an iridologist in 2005, I have studied nutrition , completing a diploma of health in 2014. I was a firm believer in the Eat Right 4Your Blood Type diet, and I went back to eating that way, but it wasn't quick enough. My energy was fading, and I needed something stronger. Thoughts of weaning were depressing me, but they felt like a necessary evil, as I was literally dragging my feet and sinking into a sadness I was very frightened to be near again.

I went to the chemist to find some supplements to boost my energy and also detox, but found that everything there wasn't safe for pregnant or breastfeeding women. *Well should we be taking it anyway?* I wondered.

At the time, I was still on Facebook (I loathe social media as a as rule, it doesn't do wonders for my anxiety AT ALL but I do appreciate it's an incredibly useful marketing too). I noticed a friend posting about her "Magic Beans." (these are Wholefood fruit, veg and berries capsules, organic, vegan and incredible for the gut-brain health link I was discovering so important to overall health and wellbeing)

I saw they were a network marketing thingy – hello, who doesn't love Tupperware? – but I wasn't scared to ask about these Magic Beans, as trusted my friend and knew she would've researched the bonkers out of them.

I was satisfied with what I found myself: the Beans were researched (in fact they are the most researched product in the world), and that they are researched by universities, which means the results aren't paid for.

These Magic Beans were ordered after a short phone conversation, and for less than a cup of coffee a day (of which I was drinking about five) I was able to afford the whole kit and caboodle.

I decided to use Frank as a test dummy (you wouldn't do the same?), and after three weeks he actually bounded into the lounge room where I was sitting.

"What's in these pills you're giving me?" he shouted, a funny smile on his face.

"Ummmm why?" I wondered if he was bleeding from his bum or something.

"Because I feel amazing! I'm getting up before my alarm every day, I've got energy, I feel really good! Oh, and my *skin*, does my skin on my face look good to you?"

I was shocked, but in a good way, and then I was pissed off – why wasn't I feeling any different?

"How do *you* feel?" he shouted gleefully.

I rang my friend, upset I wasn't feeling any of this "magic" she had promised me.

"But babe," she reassured me gently, "you're lactating; your body has been working overtime for too long. You must be really depleted, so I advise you to just double dose!"

"That's safe?" I giggled nervously, reminded of the club days, where double -dosing was fun but kind of dangerous – but now I was a mum, and double-dosing put fear into my heart.

"Yes, hon, of course! They are only made from organic fruit and veg. The Olympic athletes take up to eight of these per day!"

"Olympic athletes take these?" I was suddenly feeling very excited, and I double-dosed then and there, excited to begin fuelling my body and feeling amazing.

I double-dosed for about two weeks, and one morning I woke up at 6:00 and sat on the couch. I realised that I was feeling...awake. Then it hit me: this must be the magic she was talking about.

I was still getting frequently woken, and I hadn't bothered to stop the wine every day of the week, and I still had the Tim-Tams in the cupboard, but six weeks into taking these Magic Beans I realised I was feeling *great*.

And it only got better. More energy, better skin, and my body actually started to CRAVE vegetables! I had never eaten so much green food in my life! After five months on the free chews, my daughter, who had only eaten chicken nuggets and sausages, was reaching for baby spinach! By flooding our bodies with micronutrients, we were sending a strong message to our second brain – our gut – that this is what we wanted more of.

The best news for me was in the blood. I am a true skeptic, so I went to the doctor exactly three months after beginning the Beans, and got great results – in fact, my doctor said he'd never seen such amazing bloods. My vitamin D was high, everything was normal, and my cholesterol was the lowest he'd ever seen. He recommended halving my anti-depressants, which was huge for me.

I was still hesitant to give up my anti-depressants after the frightening year I'd had in 2014, but I realised I was starting to really feel good mentally.

We were on a family holiday and we were driving towards a theme park on a family holiday. I suddenly realised that I felt **so** healthy and *worth it* that I started to cry with happiness.

I was *sold*; these Magic Beans were incredible, and I began my own health business, encouraging pregnant and breastfeeding mothers to bridge the gap between "mum fog brain" and positive mental health. They are safe for mothers who are pregnant, breastfeeding, or have the MTHFR gene mutation, like myself and my children.

## My rise from drinking

> *God grant me the serenity to accept the things that I cannot change, the courage to change the things that I can, and the wisdom to know the difference...*

I was discovering a new problem: the cheeky wine that I was having to "relax" after the mental breakdown in 2014 was still a part of my life. After weaning my son at two (yes, I made it!), I was now a full-blown alcoholic.

I couldn't stop if I tried, I really couldn't. I would do things like get drunk on a Sunday night, so that I'd be too hungover to drink on a Monday, and hopefully, Tuesday. But by Wednesday, I'd be back at it again, drinking at lunchtime on Thursday (maybe 10 A.M.... that's nearly 12:00, isn't it?). And then of course it would be Friday again, so of course I'd be having a drink.

I'd try just drinking beer. I stopped drinking white wine. I only drank red wine. Then I'd only drink spirits, but not for long, because that was too expensive for a one-income family. I tried abstaining but would never last more than two days. I would try to have "just one," but I've honestly only ever successfully done that about three times in my life – ever.

So, I couldn't stop drinking, which meant I had to stop driving, especially as a mum. I had to walk everywhere pushing both kids in the double pram (yes, a primary school child was in the pram because I needed to do the shopping via foot as I was too drunk to drive).

My children once exclaimed loudly in the bottle shop, "Why do we come here every day, Mummy?"

I laughed with the person selling me my wine. "Well, because I'm a mummy…and mummies need wine." Ha ha ha.

We'd all laugh, secretly knowing that it was wrong, and that I needed more alcohol-free days than I was really getting. Violin classes were started and stopped, as they were on a Thursday and Mummy needed to start drinking by lunchtime on Thursdays, and the lessons were too far to walk to. "Sorry, darling, maybe you can do violin another year."

Of course, Frank didn't know quite how much I was drinking, especially during the day. I was always moaning about how I needed to stop, but he kept telling me I was overreacting, as he only witnessed a third of what I was actually ingesting.

There were many weekends when I would wake up on a Sunday morning, not recalling how I got to sleep, often wondering why I was fully-dressed – and of course, not knowing how both the kids were put to bed. I would always ask and would be surprised that most of the time *I* had put them to sleep.

"You're a great mum, even when you're pissed," Frank would often marvel. I'd cringe when he said it; I was scared at how much I was blacking out.

But it during my daughter's second school year that my life started to spiral so out of control that my personality started to change.

The beautiful connection I had so lovingly formed with my amazing children, was starting to get cracks in it.

I was still waking frequently to a teething boy of two, and my six-year-old daughter was struggling with school. I was struggling with an online business that friends were not supportive of – in fact, they were downright *unsupportive*. (I have found over the years that network marketing brings out people's inner demons. It's not a pyramid scheme, everyone, you all need to leave mums who want to earn a living from home *alone*. Or better yet, support them! They're trying to stay home with their babies!)

I was drinking so much that even whilst doing health calls with clients or teammates, I'd have a glass of red hidden in one hand and a cigarette in the other! I reached the second highest position in my health business mostly drunk – imagine what I could've done whilst sober!

It was the mornings that were changing me. Due to having a hangover almost every morning, I was very, *very* tired.

Remember, I also hadn't had a good night's sleep in six years – so I started getting CRANKY and MEAN.

I would get to bed around midnight, because most nights I was up drinking, and then cooking drunk food to soak up the alcohol, and then sometimes trying to purge so I wouldn't be drunk and/or hungover in the morning.

So, waking up to two wakeful children was very tricky on a sober day, let alone *every* day, and with a hangover. My children would get up and turn on the TV around 7:00 A.M. Actually, I have no idea if that happened, to be honest. I would wake up at 7:00 A.M. to have a hungover pee, and notice they were watching TV.

"Morning," I'd say feebly. If I wasn't too messed up, I'd make them breakfast and then go back to bed for an hour. If I was too hungover, then I'd make them breakfast, but be grumpy about it. I would moan about the noise on the TV, and otherwise wouldn't interact at all, never able to get them dressed and ready early enough to get them to school on time. My daughter was late every day.

But it was the yelling that was starting to scare me. If we were late (my fault) or my kids weren't dressed (again, my fault) I could handle it, but if my daughter didn't put her socks on quickly enough, I'd lose my temper – BADLY. And if they didn't move towards the door to leave after I'd asked them to in my Mary Poppins "I'm trying to be nice" voice, then I'd lose it and scream, "GET OUTTTTTTT!"

Fists clenched, face red, knees bent, hunched over, and screaming as loud as I could. Projecting all my self-hatred onto their beautiful little shoulders – all because I couldn't stop drinking.

And then we'd get in the car, and I'd stop, realising how I'd sounded, and I would either start crying and apologise, or apologise and then lecture them about putting their socks on more quickly, please. Then I'd buy an apology present for the oldest to give her after school and treat my son to whatever he wanted that day to be "nice mummy" for the rest of the day.

I was always miserable, which was always giving me an excuse to drink; a vicious cycle.

### A change comes

I don't know how much Frank knew of my late nights, but it was not til October 2017 when I did something that changed my life.

I don't know why I did it, but one Thursday night, I used my iPhone and filmed myself. Thursdays were a huge night for me, I don't know why, but they were. I was often already high from drinking during the day, and so the evening dinner was often rushed and for me, mainly liquid. I'd be three sheets to the wind and ducking outside all the time to "check the pool pump" and slope down the side of the house for another cigarette.

I'd then be angry at the kids for not getting to bed quickly enough, and stories were rushed and back pats were quick and in the end I'd either fume to Frank that he "do it" (amidst cries for Mummy), and I'd feel like rocking in the corner, as I just wanted to put myself into my invisible jar of alcohol.

One Friday morning, when I woke up, I saw a drunken note I'd started to write, lying on the kitchen bench. It was addressed to Frank and said – albeit illegibly – that I was a horrible person and that he shouldn't be with me.

I could barely read it, and I kind of freaked out again, as I couldn't remember writing it. I wondered what on Earth I was talking about.

Then I started going through my phone to find a photo of the kids to post another positive "health message" (ironic, of course – a positive health coach on Instagram by day, insane alcoholic by night) and stumbled across the latest photo/video in my phone. I looked at the time: it was 2:43 A.M. *Damn*, I thought. *No wonder I feel like shit.* I opened the file and froze.

It was a video of myself, talking to the camera.

My eyes are completely black, and my head was lolling about as if I was too drunk to hold it up. When I started talking, my voice was deep and shaky, and I was very, very, *VERY* drunk.

The camera wobbles a bit as I speak: "Hi Elizabeth, I just wanted to show you what you looked like when you drink, and I just wanted to show you why you *hate yourself* so much –"

I quickly pressed stop, dropped the phone, and just stared at it.

I felt my heart sink and my adrenal glands do their thing, and I felt the fight or flight response kick in – BIG TIME. Head to toe adrenaline. I felt dizzy, and if I were about to faint.

I just stared at my phone. *Who* was *that?* I thought.

I was frightened; I realised in that moment that if I didn't stop drinking, I was probably going to die. I wasn't sure how, but I knew I would, and I knew I had to stop because the amount of self-hatred in that woman's eyes absolutely terrified me.

I put away the phone and got the kids to school. I never did watch the end of that video. I was too scared to; I had only watched the first 14 seconds and it had scared me like crazy. The running was over two minutes, and I knew that if I watched it, I would be sent back to hospital and be put on medication again. So, I set into motion a plan to stop drinking, once and for all, to save my life.

Two days later I was drinking again. Not as much – in fact I only got drunk two more times after that – and this time I had a plan.

I decided that I was going to tell everyone that I was going to stop drinking, so that they would all keep me accountable and no one would offer me a drink because they all *knew* I wasn't drinking. My excuse? I was going to run a marathon.

Now I am actually someone that enjoys fun runs. My personal claim to fame is doing the Run for Kids in Melbourne whilst pushing my son in a pram the whole 15.7 kilometres. I've done many five and 10K runs, and a marathon has always been on the cards. But this time, it was my excuse to stop having people offer me a drink.

I hoped that by the end of the year, people would be so used to me not drinking, that I could continue my sobriety and they wouldn't question me. Because I knew it couldn't be "just a year" – it had to be forever. I could never drink again. Those black eyes haunted me; they still do. It is called a "gift of desperation" to remain sober.

I started spreading the word. It was a feasible excuse, and everyone bought it. It made a lot of sense, in fact: here I was running a health business, of COURSE I'd run a marathon. I must be soooo healthy that it will be easy! Ha!

Because my drinking was so heavy, I hadn't run more than three times that year. I'd tell Frank I was going to the gym, and I would, but I'd ride the bike for 10 minutes and then go to the bottle shop.

I'd buy more than I said I would, hide one bottle in the car and then take one inside. Then, when Frank was having his nightly shower, I'd quickly drink the rest of bottle number one and replace it with bottle number two.

And so, it comes to the end of the year. We arrange a New Year's Eve party, and my best friend Sarah arrives the day before.

*The last hurrah*

I lay next to my daughter on the lounge room as she watches a movie with her brother and a friend's son. The adults, some of whom have travelled more than three hours to visit us, are all outside drinking.

I had come inside to refill my glass of wine and noticed the bored look on my big girl's face as she watched a movie more designed to please the two younger humans in the room, purely because they complain louder than she does. She's just turned seven, and she seems so wise and adult now. Just like her mother, the weight of the world sits on her shoulders and every emotion twinkles in her beautiful brown eyes, but she has the bored look of resentment on her beautiful little face.

Mummy is not drunk yet, or else she probably wouldn't have noticed this bored look. I go over to her and lay down to cuddle her. I face her, probably breathing wine breath all over her face. She very politely says nothing.

"Guess what?" I say, looking into her eyes, which light up.

*Is she expecting a present?* My kids do tend to be spoiled when I drink; I can be found fishing out lollies and chips and hidden trinkets that I've spent lavishly on to drown out the guilt singing in my ears as I buy extra wine for the parties I insist on having, all the while attempting to fulfil the narrative in my head about the role I'm playing as a mother in a marriage I insist on trying to save.

"What?" she sounds bored, but her eyes give her away.

"Mummy's not going to drink wine next year."

My girl looks at me with a quiet, disbelieving expression. She waits.

I say it again, this time with expression for dramatic effect: "For a WHOLE year…NO alcohol!"

"Not even beer?" she asks, obviously in tune with Mummy's drinking struggles over the last two years.

"Not even beer." I say this in a voice meant to convince both the receiver *and* the giver. I have my wits about me somewhat and can sense that the little girl is doubting me, worried to some degree about my drinking – and *that* is a worry in itself.

"Yay!" she cries and cuddles me. Hard. Fiercely. With anxious love

As the night progresses, she brings it up a few more times, with joy, reassuring both of us that my promise of No Alcohol is really going to happen.

"So, you're really not drinking next year?"

"No, darling."

"No more wine next year, really?"

"I said NO, honey. Go watch the rest of the movie"

I play on the attention, marvelling at how happy it makes my daughter, but later reflecting on how shit it makes me feel to reflect on such conversations between a mother and child.

"Oh yes, Mummy's going to play with you MUCH more next year!"

My daughter: "Not even red wine?"

Me: "Not even sparkly bubbly wine my love...OMG its going to be sahhhhhhhhh ahmayzing to be playing with yewwwwww."

By the end of the night it's drunk cigarette breath, plastered on my daughter and son's faces, stumbling in and out of the lounge room, fading in and out of the children's existence with bowls of chips, lollies, soft drink and chocolate – all the things children simply don't need at 10:00 at night!

But I am feeling like I'm loving them, even though I'm just trying to fade out the guilt that I am drunk once again and knowing that I behave like an idiot when I'm drunk.

Nice Drunk Mummy goes to sleep, and Mummy fades into the blackness. The kids are forgotten altogether, and all that's important is filling the darkness in her heart by drinking herself into oblivion.

The entitled girl, all her insecurities about what she is doing with herself, unleashed into a glass of wine and a night of pretending she is in her 20s again. Drinking excessively, because she knows she is powerless to change anything except the song in the CD player.

*I can't change now*, she thinks. *It's all too late*. She's 40 years old and just a drunk mum.

Cue darkness, the usual blackout ending the night for her at God knows what time.

*The next morning*

I wake up with, you guessed it, a mother of a hangover (pun intended – yes, you see what I did there). And when I wake up in my bed, completely clothed, and completely unsure how or when I got there, and completely unsure where the kids are, I am relieved it's still 2017.

Because I am stopping drinking in 2018, and the only thing that will take care of this massive hangover is more wine. I quickly apply some make up, make coffees for everyone, and give the kids some reassuring hugs. I didn't mean it – didn't mean what? Oh you know, forgetting about you and getting drunk, that's all. And then THE self-hatred looms in me like a storm).

"I'm sorry I'm a bad mum!" I say, completely meaning it and yet trying to cover up the pain of it in a song and a joke. I even sing this to myself in the kitchen, as I attempt to be the Hostess with the Mostest and cook breakfast for everyone so as to not feel like a shit person: *Bad mum, Bad mum, Whatcha gonna do? Whatcha gonna do when the bad mum's YOU?*

I sneak a glance to see if my daughter is listening. *I want her to feel my guilt*, I think. *I want her to know that I know I'm feeling bad. I want her to know I know I'm letting her down.*

*But really*, I rationalise with myself again, my sober judgmental mind realising I am trying to manipulate a child's feelings, *is it her position to understand any of this? She's only seven years old, for goodness' sake, woman!*

The dads aren't as hungover as the mums and so the kids get palmed off on them. They all go fishing whilst us mums go and get our nails done. It is to be my last night drinking alcohol, and I mean to make myself the Queen of the Evening. Nails done, alcohol bought, and food prepared.

Surprisingly I decide to go out on beers – a whole slab, of course, because I don't want to get drunk too quickly, which wine would do. I intend on pacing myself for the last-ever night of Drunken Glory.

The kids are tired from the night before (thankfully for them – Monster Mummy wouldn't be happy if they screwed up her last night on the piss!), so the mums don't need to be inside all the time.

The evening is actually tamer than the night before, as everyone is slightly dusty from last night's raucous excitement, so it's just beer after beer, and kids put in bed well before midnight.

Nice Mummy is still in the house, so she manages to get them asleep in a relatively loving fashion, and she is surprised at how smoothly the night is going. The group decides that after midnight, I can continue drinking, even though it's technically 2018 – why not just finish up the night? "After all, you *deserve* it," they all say.

An enabler's last words. In the eyes of an addict, any excuse is a great one. One drink is too many, and a thousand never enough.

Soon it's early morning, about 3:00 A.M., and some guests are starting to leave. I start to get angry at them.

*How dare they leave? It's my last night!* I fume.

But they leave anyway, and I think *Eff you, I'm going to keep drinking*. The party is started again by rolling some green. It's now 5:00 A.M. and the music is still blaring.

The next parts I don't remember. In fact, I don't actually really recall the entire night, but this next bit is true blackness.

I am standing in front of the pool in my long, black, flowing dress, and I fall backwards in slow motion, down, down, down, into the swimming pool....

Like a mad woman's baptism, it's as if I am rebirthing myself at the end of the drinking madness. My friend helps to pull me out of the pool, fully clothed and soaking wet.

It's now 7:00 A.M. and I stumble into the kitchen. At the same time, my daughter comes around the doorway, swinging her toy monkey. The toy swings straight into my face, and its hard plastic eyes connect perfectly with my bloodshot, mascara-stained ones.

I scream: "I can't see! I can't see!"

I drop onto the kitchen floor and my little girl bursts into tears. Sarah tells her calmly to "go get Daddy," and tries unsuccessfully to get me up off the kitchen floor.

When Frank comes, I am scooped up and taken to my son's room to "sleep it all off."

Meanwhile, Sarah sits in my daughter's bed, cuddling both her and my son, who are crying because their mother is now blind. She consoles them by reading them stories.

I wake up in a panic, with the familiar *Where am I?* blood rush, and realise I'm in my son's bedroom.

It's 2:35 P.M., and I can't remember anything past 11:00 the night before.

*What did I do? What time is it? Why is my hair wet?*

Without even checking in or saying hello to anyone, I jump into the shower – to wash away all of the bad memories and try to piece the night together.

The shower does not evoke any memories and I realise I'm going to have to face the music. The blackout still lingers in my mind, and I am nervous and anxious.

*What did I do?* I remember this phrase as one I have moaned for many, many years of my life. Waking up naked, waking up to plates of half-eaten food, waking up dressed in different clothes, waking up with the stove on, waking up with my face scraped off...so many mornings of pain and darkness.

And the insanity of doing it again, and again, and again. I lean my head against the shower wall, staring at my legs and trying to feel my soul.

*It's not there*, I think. I drank it to death.

I give up trying to remember the night before and get out of the shower. I try to look myself in the mirror, but I can't. Looking in the mirror is very hard – the self-hatred in the life of an alcoholic is huge, and the solution is always to just drink yourself into blackness. It's a cycle of revenge on yourself, which seems perfectly rational at the time. But as the years progress, and your self-hatred consumes you, it filters into your everyday life – in fact, it IS your everyday life! And you isolate yourself, so that no one can see just how much you wish you were dead.

It's a shameful walk into the kitchen, to avoid the people sitting in the lounge room. But I am caught by my family.

I give a sheepish smile, "Well then, no more alcohol for Mummy."

The response is silence. I wonder, mortified at myself, *What have I just put my children through?*

But my husband and friends smile at me kindly and ask politely how I feel. I decide to feed the troops, and as I begin to do so, I realise my daughter hasn't spoken to me yet, and I feel a rush of dread.

*Oh no*, I think, *I've finally ruined it. What the hell did I do?*

The recollection of that midnight promise in 2010 to my newborn daughter to "get my shit together," and then not being able to actually do it, sweeps through my mind and has me buckle at my knees.

Even now I wonder if I can actually get my shit together. What if I've ruined our relationship? I seek her out, just as she is bravely seeking out me. Oh that little girl, she is so brave!

We meet in the doorway of the kitchen and the little darling has her head hanging. I grab her tightly in a HUGE hug, a hug of guilt and shame and love. She speaks first, quietly saying, "I'm sorry, Mummy."

I stop and hold her back at arm's length, confused. I try to meet her eyes, but my daughter's head continues to hang, and I realise she is actually apologising to me!

"What for?" I gasp. I'm horrified that this is what I've turned into, an emotional blackmailer. I'm mortified that a seven-year-old is apologising to a 40-year-old drunk. What the hell did I say to her? What bullshit lies did I spin to make her feel so terrible that she feels she needs to take responsibility for any of this?

I continue to hold her tight, her face pressed into my tummy. The feeling is dreadful. The guilt is humungous, but mainly, I feel sad. Sad that I have been given the responsibility to be this beautiful girl's mummy and that I've let her down so much.

"Because of the monkey."

"What monkey?" Of course I don't remember a thing.

"My white monkey..." She explains what happened, and then she starts to cry.

*Oh, what a stupid mum you are*, I think, abusing myself freely. *You stupid idiot, why couldn't you just get your self together seven years ago?! You don't deserve her!*

I hold my daughter tight and try hard not to bawl my eyes out. "I thought I'd made you blind," she says, full of grief and continuing to cry.

I console her and am saddened to note that I actually feel relief! I even make a point of telling the others what has happened: "The monkey! She hit me in the eye with the monkey."

"Ohhhhhhhh..."

I think there is a sense relief from the other adults, too, because for a small amount of time, the other adults actually didn't know why I was lying on the kitchen floor, screaming that I was blind. They honestly just thought I'd lost my shit.

*Which I actually have*, I muse disappointedly to myself. I am so ashamed of myself that I'm nearly sick.

"Oh, baby girl," I say, "it was an accident! I'm OK!"

The hug continues, until I realise the girl has stopped crying and she wishes to move forward with the day and try to move on past this awful moment. So, I address the rest of the room: "I'm sorry if I upset anyone, it was all just an accident. And luckily, this won't happen again."

I pause to gauge responses. The other adults look at me kindly…they are being so kind! Or are they just really hungover too?

I give my daughter one last squeeze, and it is a long and hard one. I hope like heck it's not too late for her to feel her mother's love and to forgive her. I wipe away her tears.

I make myself a coffee.

And Sober. The Heck. Up.

## *Sobriety*

January 2, 2018. The official "day 1" of being sober.

I wake up without a hangover. Sort of. Actually, I feel like shit still. I didn't drink last night, aren't I meant to be feeling better? I pretend I feel amazing, and I kind of brag a lot about it, asking, "Coffee, anyone?" in the most cheerful of voices. Maybe too cheerful. Yes, too cheerful. The self-loathing begins: *F@#$ you, you stupid bitch. What the hell have you done to yourself?*

I stand at the kitchen bench, waiting for the coffee to make itself, and I nearly break down. A small tear runs down my face and I angrily wipe it away.

*This is on you*, I say to myself. *You deserve to feel like shit. You don't deserve for your kids to love you, and you can just get your shit together for once in your dumb life.*

The abuse is really hard, and yet I actually find solace in it over the next few weeks, like a martyr. It keeps me from crying every 10 minutes.

The shame and the guilt are like two separate entities in the room – they almost need to move into the spare room, they are that big to me. I shower with them, make them breakfast, and take them to bed with me. They follow me around, and if I'm not careful, they push me to my knees and make me cry.

My daughter is suspicious. I mean, I don't blame her, but it's like having the Spanish inquisition follow me around, and for days – months, in fact – I am constantly reassuring her that what is in my cup or glass isn't alcohol. Many times I just show her. Like I said, I don't blame her, but it's extra fuel for the shame and guilt entities.

I firstly start to detox – wow. It's almost instant: day one, I go to the toilet and what comes out is black, runny, and shakes me to the core. I am confused, scared, and mostly worried. *What had I done to myself?*

I sit on the toilet and put my head into my shaking hands. I stare at the tiles for what seems like hours (I know its only minutes, a child would've come looking for me if it was too long), and I see monster's faces within the patterns of the tiles, and feel I've descended into Hell.

I've heard about this, this thing called detox. It's reserved for the addicts and alcoholics amongst us. Surely I don't fit that bill? Is this really me?

I moan at the cramps, and the diarrhea that oozes from my shaking body. My stomach folds neatly onto my thighs and it reminds me of being pregnant – only

I'm not. I'm just carrying the sugar from a thousand drinks around my middle, and it's seemingly trying to make its way out in one sitting. I nearly let myself cry again, but I'm too in shock. Someone who is qualified to write you a nutritional program to have you glowing from the back of your teeth, runs a health and wellness business, has a diploma of health...and here I am, a Living Lie.

Unhealthy. Groaning with pain. Shamefully detoxing. But alive.

I admonish myself again, swearing, and then I wipe it away. And wipe. And wipe.

The days of detox have begun. I shake for about nine days. I have diarrhea for about 14. I feel dizzy for three weeks. And then, after the distraction of the physical symptoms end, in comes the emotions – with a Capital E.

Real. Raw. Like I haven't been felt in years, Emotions, dropping into the mothership of my brain like suicide bombers, every day. They are relentless. It is the End of Days, every day, and there's no sign of a white flag being flown.

In fact, the emotions become like entities, too, or like minefield bombs, ready to blow up if I turn the wrong corner and step on one.

I actually start to turn corners slowly. I'll be walking through the house, feeling like *I've got this*, ready to put in a load of washing...and BAM!

Like a karate chop to the neck, an emotion is there to bash me up! I will stand there, crying, unsure what has hit me and unsure what to do, except stand there and cry. I feel the emotion move through me as I continue with the washing. By the time I hang the clothes out, I am literally bawling my eyes out, deep in a feeling I cannot figure out.

I don't know what to do about them, nor do I know how to behave with them, so I just learn to move through them. Paying attention only because I have to out of sheer pain. I have no, strategy except to continue to live and I hope they will go away along with the shakes, the sweats, and the shits.

And love handles. I'm a slim girl, but these pockets of fat are well and truly entrenched on my hips, in the way that only bottles and bottles of wine can create. I vainly look daily at my muffin tops and hold on for the day I wake up and they are just gone.

After a month of these feelings pouncing on me, I decide to switch the witch for the bitch and find a new addiction: studying. I throw myself into my exam preparation which I will be sitting in early May. But all this does is delay the bombs – and trust me, they are coming to get me.

*The End and the Beginning*

Now I'm 7 months sober and needing to take the path that isn't the same one as my husband. The marriage ends and the kids and I move into a unit across town.

The point of this next section isn't to talk about the divorce (the healing is monumental, and we do the best we can to end it with ease grace and flow, but it's not easy) – the point of this small chapter is that the solution to my healing from drinking is life-changing. I am given a Holy Spirit Bible by a good friend. "Thanks," I say, but I think, *Why?*

For some reason, however, I eventually decide to read it. It is a teaching Bible with exercises in it, and, unusually for me, I decide to actually read it properly start doing the exercises.

Soon I am doing prayer exercises every day. On week 3, it tells me to write a prayer, asking the Holy Spirit something. I write this: *I pray for you to show me what I need to do, and where I need to be to be able to heal completely. For the health and safety of me and my children.*

That same day, I drive one child to school and take the other to the chiropractor on the other side of town On the way back, I find myself driving down a side street, and pulling up beside the back entrance to the cinemas in Geelong. I feel as if I'm being led there.

Suddenly, I realise I am outside the Wesley Centre. I realise it's a Monday. I look at the clock: it's mid-morning. I look up at the sky.

"Oh," I say to God whilst, putting all of this information together, "You want me THERE, do you?"

A few years earlier, whilst doing my health business I met with a customer who said she was an art therapist for drug addicts, and also that she helped women go through the 12 steps to get off drugs and alcohol. I'd been keen, as I was recognising early signs of my drinking going off the rails, and I even went to a few meetings. (It was 2016, and once I heard the word "relapse" I thought, *Oh goodie, I can just relapse for a few more months...*)

There was a women's Narcotics Anonymous meeting going on and I was 100% certain that I had been led to it meeting by the Holy Spirit.

So, I went in. I was a regular there, for the better half of the year. The following year, I started my own meetings on Thursday afternoons. Women only, and recovery-focused, and next thing you know I was finding myself a higher power (God).

It's all well and good to stop drinking, because drinking causes health and emotional problems. But while you are drinking, you are not dealing with anything; you are not living. You are just drinking away your problems, which actually don't go anywhere. They lay dormant in your body, until you stop drinking, and then they all have to come up to the surface, ready for you to deal with them!

This can be very scary and depressing, and can threaten to push you into a darkness which may very well have you drinking again – unless you do something about it, like attending a recovery fellowship like AA or NA.

The Global fellowships of AA and NA are incredible, the recovery rate is very high especially if you focus on the 12 steps. This is very important, if you are attending AA. Here's what I love about the 12 steps: they are attached with a promise – if you follow the steps, honestly and with vigour, then you will be free from the addiction to drugs and alcohol. I find that absolutely incredible, how a book (*The Big Book*) actually has a *promise* of a solution.

## Finding God

The story of my journey to find God is deeply personal. I can only share this: it is one that has helped me live a beautiful life that is free from addiction, alcohol, anger, and frustration.

I am not the mother that screams at her children anymore. During that first year of sobriety, I worked and worked and worked on myself – through prayer, meditation and counselling – to STOP SCREAMING. By the end of 2018, I was a scream-free Mother.

By the end of 2019, I had developed the breastfeeding meditations and recorded them. I had even written most of this book. But I spent most of those years not just healing myself from the separation and later divorce, but also healing with my children. I never took my eyes off of them, ensuring I put procedures and processes into my home life to help us remain calm and relaxed (such as a routine, like Friday night movie night, Sunday pizza night, and nightly prayer and back scratches). No more rocking in the corner trying to get the kids to sleep – bedtimes are so easy now, and enjoyable!

I also got them help in the way of art therapy, social workers. and lots of nurturing and love.

Wine had interfered with my life so much that it was like meeting my kids all over again. But I felt like I had gotten my babies back.

Thank GOD I was doing all of this sober.

I can happily say that I am now a completely changed woman, and proudly into my fourth year of sobriety.

I don't ever crave alcohol, I have a wonderful relationship with my children and their father, and I live a purposeful life. I am enjoying being sober and I am enjoying having a relationship with a God of my own understanding, a loving Creator that loves me for who I am.

I don't have to pretend to be anyone other than me, and my children see me the way I imagine God does, with unconditional and pure love. They are the most incredible gifts from above, and I love rising daily to be the very best sober and calm Mummy that I can possibly be.

If you need help with your drinking, then jump onto the AA website (aa.org) and search for a meeting near you.

It works if you work it, so work it – you're worth it.

## Chapter 2.

# R!SE MOTHER R!SE
# (L!STEN TO YOUR BABY & BREASTFEEDING GUIDE)

I'm standing in the hallway in my dressing gown, head pressed against the wall. It's 3:00 A.M., *I think*. I cannot remember if I just went to my baby, or if I am on my way back to her. I decide to just wait in the hallway, and my eyes start to close...I drift off.

She cries again and my head jerks up. My forehead is sore, and I don't know how long I've been asleep standing up, my tired head pressed hard against the plaster. I go to her quickly, noting how awake I am all of a sudden, and I pick her up, anxious to soothe her cries. Careful to hold her – "don't drop her" thoughts swirling instinctively in my brain – I sit down on the hard wooden rocking chair.

I sit down and fumble to release my tingling breast (my let down is strong in the early weeks), my beautiful something-week-old baby is searching for me and, for her beloved "mummy's milk." Balancing her on my lap and still fumbling to lift up my top, unclip my bra, and take out the wet breast pads, and all with only two hands.

*I'm so uncoordinated*, I fume. *Why am I wearing so many clothes?"*

Immediately I start to compare myself with what the newspapers and magazines say I should be doing. Surely, she should be in her own room by now, and sleeping through the night. "Put her down," the "experts" say. "Stop holding her so much." "Just give her a bottle, she'll sleep longer."

I feel…I don't know how to feel right now. Maybe its guilt? Am I doing this all wrong? Am I ruining my baby by attending to her cries?

So many people keep telling me to let her cry and that then she'll sleep, but my body and my heart simply *cannot* do that to her. My anxiety to keep her from crying is an unrecognised early motherly instinct, and my instincts are stronger than what I am, but I don't recognise them that way during these early months. As a new mother, I question absolutely everything.

I love her so much, and I just want to do the best I can – and it seems ridiculous to let a newborn baby keep crying. Logical thinker and emotionally available person that I naturally am, I deduce that if there are tears, then there needs to be attention. This is a human baby, the most helpless species of all the species on Earth! I simply cannot let her cry without picking her up and feeding her or cuddling her.

But the self-doubt intrudes on my midnight meetings with my little angel. Societal demands that I am meant to be getting a full night's sleep are intruding on our family happiness, and questions are being raised as to why I'm still "so tired" still.

But hallway sleeping was never mentioned in the hospital, and again I think to myself, "Maybe I'm doing it all wrong."

I finally release my breast from the seemingly endless amount of clothes I am wearing, and she latches on instantly...and perfectly.

And then, everything disappears, and time stands still.

It's just her and I.

I sigh. I forget all about the judgements, the tiredness, the confusion, and the bloody hard rocking chair, and I enjoy the breastfeeding bliss.

"This. Is. Where. I. Am," my soul reminds me.

"This. Is. Who. You. Are," my heart sings to me. "There is nowhere else you should be right now, no place on the face of the Earth except here, feeding your daughter. No one you need to please, except this tiny baby girl." Amen to that.

During that beautiful moment of clarity I take all of her in with my loving new eyes,: her perfect little face, her spiky brown hair, her tiny little fists, her tiny little feet, her innocence nurtured at my breast and in my arms, with only the simple act of feeding her to placate her and make absolutely everything in her world be OK. I realise that this is the first time in my life that all I need to do is to exist, and by the sheer action of existing, for her I am *everything*.

I take another deep breath and enjoy the rest of the feed. Slowly, I start to take note of the bliss amongst the chaos – and not just in this instance, but over the next few months. I stop listening to everyone else and instead choose to listen to my baby – which makes me listen to myself. Her tears force me to listen to how I am as a person, and her inability to do anything for herself forces me to become someone new.

I was a lost self-doubting girl who knew exactly who she wasn't, until I had a baby, and then I realised that I was found – as a mother. A part of me was born alongside my baby, and it is the part of me that is woman, that is whole, that is wild, that is incredibly strong, and that is incredibly full of Love.

I am a mother.

The bond I gained with my daughter through breastfeeding was incredibly strong and incredibly nurturing. I felt as nurtured by the close contact as she did, feeding her every two hours around the clock. The constant feeding took much mental effort on my behalf, yet felt intrinsically simple to carry out physically, and I navigated the constant negative "helpful" advice from family and friends regarding her wakefulness.

My insistence on living out the routine as she demanded it, eventually meant that I needed to find evidence as to why I felt that what I was doing was normal, natural, and exactly what she needed. I needed to convince objecting family that what I was doing was right for *her*. Her well-being came first – I just needed to find the information to support my actions, so that I could grow in confidence.

So, I started talking to people about breastfeeding. I felt that the key to my baby's well-being here was to elongate the breastfeeding relationship, not stop it, which was the first thing many health professionals and family members advised me to do, so that she would "sleep better." I felt certain, deeply within my core, that the emotional connection I was feeling with her was not just reciprocated but *essential* to her development. I also felt that breastmilk *had* to be better than man-made alternatives. I had been "awakened" to food by then and so was already following the simple theory, "If you can't read the ingredients, then your body probably cannot process it!" I felt these things were way more important for her than having her sleep by herself in a room down the hallway, just so that I could get a full eight hours sleep, too.

So, after a referral from a mother's group, I contacted the Australian Breastfeeding Association (ABA) . I didn't feel I had any issues with breastfeeding per se, but the regular feeds every two hours weren't slowing down, and my baby was now right months old. Family and friends were practically screaming at me to give her a bottle, and I hadn't quite learned the art of navigating advice yet. (Nowadays I have the confidence to pull it off, but back then, I struggled for my instincts to as a mother to heard and respected.)

The phone call to the ABA changed my life. The counsellor didn't even say anything profound at all, it was the reassurance that what I was doing was normal, natural and *exactly* what my baby needed, that hit home. She reassured me immensely that I wasn't breaking my baby by loving and holding her!

You may be surprised that the breastfeeding itself had little to do with the what changed my direction as a mother. Really, it was the permission to *hold my baby* that made the most difference: picking up a baby was actually OK, and in doing so, I was not spoiling her, I was advancing her emotional connections, and attending to her innocent needs.

The human baby is the most helpless of all mammals, and crying is their only way of knowing if they are being cared for. In the first couple of months, they cannot see very well, and they need to feel that they are with their caregiver...so it makes perfect sense that they need to be held! (When I did it the second time around, with my son, I just didn't bother putting him down, and he actually became independent from me more quickly, because his emotional needs were met so absolutely from the day he was born.)

From the very first ABA meeting, I was *empowered* to feed my baby for as long as we wanted to continue doing so. (Note: breastfeeding is a relationship, just like any other, and if one party in the relationship isn't happy, then the relationship needs assistance and possibly needs to end altogether. I have often helped friends wean instead of continuing to pursue breastfeeding because the relationship was not mutual, and this is better than feeding your baby "emotionally toxic" breastmilk).

After my first meeting, I went straight to the group leader and asked to sign up to become a counsellor, knowing that my new knowledge on all things breastfeeding would become my super-power.

In just under a year I qualified, and I am excited to share the information and experiences I have gained with you. As you saw in the dedication, this book is for all mothers, and I hope to "normalise" certain experiences that I myself struggled with in my journey as a mother.

I wish to encourage you to listen to your gut, the motherly instincts that are truly born the day your baby arrives. The instincts that certain narratives and health professionals are even still somewhat blind to or in denial about helping you tap into. I wish to impart the wisdom of the many years of counselling I have done, with well over a thousand mothers, to assist you with "normal" issues.

And yes, issues with breastfeeding are "normal," so don't feel pressure to give up just because there is a hurdle. I wish to empower you and open your eyes to the methods I have used to mentally and physically tap into my motherly instincts, the tools that have enabled me to form an incredible connection with my children, and step into the shoes of the woman and mother of substance I so lovingly see in the mirror every day.

In all things spiritual, we refer to the Holy trinity of our existence as being intertwined with each other, mind, body and soul. You cannot achieve balance in life until you pay attention to all three.

This made so much sense to me, and when I started my business helping mothers breastfeed, I called it Mind, Body, and Milk.

Milk is the soul of a parenting journey. Breastfeeding is not just about breastfeeding. It's not just about "feeding" your baby; it's one of the deepest ,most loving acts a human being can do for another.

Aside from making love, nothing is as sacred as having a baby nurture from your very body. Transferring your nutrients from you to them. It's not called liquid gold for nothing, and the emotional connection you BOTH feel lasts for as long as you both live.

I will soon explain what is in breast milk, and why it's important to feed, for nutritional, emotional, and environmental reasons. But the reasons – especially today, as I write this amongst a muzzled society – are even more important, as society and technology are encouraging us to keep apart and only communicate via phones or computers. The simple joys of having a hug are lost, and the physical touch that we as a species absolutely NEED, is gone. So, to be here, encouraging women to breastfeed their children, is quite simply, the most important thing I can think to do in this time.

It is in losing yourself that you are found, (I believe this is what Jesus told his disciples), and I have found that by giving myself over and over again to the role of mother, I have found myself, again and again.

I have found her in places I didn't think possible: in the pantry, pumping milk from my bosom to ease engorgement; in the 2:00 A.M. fever-watch, anxiously checking my baby's temperature every half hour; in the baby change rooms at shopping centres (who knew these places even existed?!); in the window of the shops when I see her reflection pushing the pram and realising its me, as Mother; hastily changing a poo explosion in the carpark, getting it all over my own clothes and ultimately aborting the shopping mission; crying on the side of the highway because, well, baby hates longs drives and mum can't stretch her boob into the back seat, so constant stops to feed baby need to happen; weaning baby and realising I was ready to do so; and stepping comfortably into the skin of the true woman I was always meant to be: a mother.

When I was beginning to research why I needed to continue to breastfeed, despite the cries of "Oh, you must stop now; she's old enough to take the bottle…" I was struck to learn that breastfeeding is referred to as "species specific" humans. Species – that word really struck a chord with me. It made me sink into the mother wolf inside of me. *I am a mammal*, I thought logically, *so it makes jolly good sense to be feeding my children as an animal would: with my body.*

But it was the spiritual connection that deepened the passion. Again and again, when I had a let down I would feel that rush of oxytocin (the hormone that triggers milk from the breast) and I would have a deepened sense of love, and deepened sense of my new purpose as a mother.

"Here," my soul would laugh, "is where you are!"

"Here!" my soul would cry. "Is who you are!"

"Here," my soul would firmly state, "is all you need to be."

So, once I commenced my journey into becoming all things breastfeeding by training to be a counsellor, I set myself on a slightly insane mission: to save the world, one boob at a time.

When you have gone through the birth (however you have gotten through it), your new baby is usually put onto your chest. You look into your baby's eyes and you really, truly SEE another soul looking at you. Not a mini-YOU or a mini-ME, you are looking at a brand-new SOUL. By acknowledging them as **a-**part *from* you, as well as a part *of* you, you begin a contract of life-long respect.

Really tuning in to them as the new and unique little human being that they are will help you to tap into their own little set of instructions. You just need to watch and learn them.

One of the most important things to know about breastfeeding is that it is natural, which means that you and baby have instincts that will help steer you towards this relationship. There may be things that impede this, but the most common factors that trips people up are lack of support towards breastfeeding and lack of information.

Listening to your baby and feeding on demand, is truly the key to beginning your relationship with your child. This "listening" is born here, and I promise you, those skills are imperative to having a close relationship with anyone, and really cementing that bond that most parents dream of having with their children.

So, regardless of what type of birth you have, that first breastfeed and skin-to -kin moment is the one that imprints their smell on you (and partner, too), and it's incredibly important that you relay to the people assisting you with your birth, that they put your baby straight onto your chest, amniotic fluid and all (pending a medical emergency, of course).

That first breastfeed is an opportunity for your baby to imprint on you. "Imprinting" is where the amniotic/birthing fluid is rubbed from your baby onto your chest. The baby will then start exploring his outside "home," putting his fist on your chest/breast, and then into his mouth, and then crawling towards your breast, creating a trail from the amniotic fluid as they crawl and sense their way.

This is also where *you* imprint on your baby. The skin to skin will elicit oxytocin, the love hormone, and you will use your outer senses – touch, sight, and hearing – to connect with your new baby.

This is a sacred time with mother and child, and should be protected at all costs. The time it can take a newborn baby to reach the breast can be up to 90 minutes. After that time, perhaps you can help baby reach the breast. And there is NO NEED (unless medically necessary – and even then, ask questions) to remove a baby from the mother's breast for at least three years to! The only reason would be to cuddle the mum's partner – that's it. Babies need to be on Mum, and society needs to shut the front door and stop pushing mums to put their babies down, get into shape, and go back to work.

The baby should have a good first feed on both sides. (Remember, you only have colostrum here, and this is practically liquid gold. The amount of nutrients in this stuff is insane – it has even been used for cancer research. More information about what is IN breastmilk follows.) Then it's time for your partner to have their "first feed." Partners, this is your chance to unbutton your own "birthing shirt" for this very moment, where you too get to imprint with your baby.

Please hold that naked baby to your bare chest for as long as you can (up to an hour or until baby needs another feed) the amniotic fluid will also imprint the birthing smell on your chest, and you will have the same oxytocin experience, and your senses of touch, sight, and hearing will bond you to your baby. This post-birth bonding is incredibly SACRED and should never be halted or disrupted by anyone, unless a life-threatening situation arises, so please ensure you put this on your instructions to whomever is assisting you with your birth.

So, what happens if you have a caesarean? OK, well this actually happened: after I was teaching a breastfeeding workshop, a keen young couple who wished to have a completely drug-free and natural birth, ended up having an emergency C-section. Due to the workshop explaining the importance of the first breastfeed, Dad got to be the facilitator of this first feed, and all-important bonding experience between the baby and mother! Mum was medically "out of it" after the surgery, but Dad, who was a supportive partner and parent, placed their baby on her chest and guided that baby to its first breastfeed. Isn't that powerful?

Both parents told me they were so grateful to have learned the importance of the first breastfeed prior to giving birth. Dad was humbled to be able to facilitate the first one, thus destroying the concept that it's all about the mum when it comes to breastfeeding

Breastfeeding is incredibly important, but it cannot be enjoyed to its full fruition if your partner isn't on board. My aim here is to demonstrate the importance of both parents' roles post-birth, and to show you methods to create an inclusive parenting relationship, especially one that fosters a healthy breastfeeding journey.

The bond that you will BOTH have with your baby after the first breastfeed lasts a lifetime. So even if it cannot be straight after the birth for medical reasons – and my second child was in special care nursery for four days post birth, so I actually lived this! – you make up for it as soon as you can. I was *still* doing skin-to-skin (tummy to tummy) up until he was 24 months old, just to calm him down and reassure him. I highly recommend to have skin-to-skin time every day.

Important benefits of skin-to-skin for Baby:

- Stabilises their heart rate
- Regulates their breathing
- Improved oxygen saturation levels
- No cold stress, more temperature stability
- Longer periods of sleep, whilst skin to skin
- More rapid weight gain
- Less caloric expenditures
- More rapid brain development
- Reduction of "purposeless activity," such as flailing of arms and legs
- Decreased crying
- Longer periods of alertness
- More successful breastfeeding episodes
- Increased breastfeeding duration

Important benefits of skin-to-skin for parents:

- Increased bonding because of increased serum oxytocin levels
- Promotes confidence in the parent's caregiving
- Increased feeling of being "in control"
- Relief of parental stress over having an infant being taken "away" from them due to birth trauma, and or medical need to remove from parent for any length of time
- Increased maternal milk production

So, the BIG question: how do you actually breastfeed?

Just like trying to drive a car blindfolded, breastfeeding can be frightening and very overwhelming. And just like all the different makes and models of cars, no two babies or breasts are the same. We are all *so* individual, it seems impossible that there would be a method that could work for everyone.

The joy of baby-led attachment is that there is honestly a solution for every single individual. Anyone who has experienced positioning and attachment not going right, knows the pain of raw, cracked nipples and the internal cacophony of swearwords pinging around your brain when trying to get baby to latch on correctly.

There *is* a way for breastfeeding to be an easy, natural, and beyond beautiful bonding experience between you and your baby. But we must remember, even when you were learning to drive your car, there were bumps along the road, right? There were moments where you thought to yourself, *There is NO way I'm going to be able to do this.* But once everything falls into place, you're cruising on easy street! Let's talk about the method that the Australian Breastfeeding recommends as the most normal and natural and easiest for baby.

**Baby-Led Attachment**

This is where the mother is seated on the bed, laying back in a semi-reclining position, well-supported, and comfortable. Baby is dressed in a nappy only, and is placed with its cheek on the mother's bare chest. The baby's body rests entirely on the mother, and the baby is left to self-attach. This is the optimal feeding position, as it encourages the baby's natural breastfeeding instincts and works well with mothers who have been struggling with the latch-on. Unfortunately, most Mums feel as though the baby is going to fall off, and it doesn't feel natural at all.

May I just pop in an opinion right now about the overload now out there on the information superhighway – the good old Internet. There are many GREAT books and articles regarding practically anything you wish to learn about; however (!), there are also lots that are NOT. Regardless of whether some mummas have good intentions, many of their posts, especially regarding breastfeeding, can actually be dangerous for a new mother to try. This information can throw off your inner compass, and the noisy overwhelm of information makes it's become harder to hear the soft quiet voice trying to lead you.

This quiet voice is your *instinct*; it is a voice or a feeling, and most of us feel it in our stomach – this is often the voice many refer to as God. Hands up – who nested as though their life depended on it when they were preggers? That right there is your motherly instincts kicking in, ladies. We have been given our very own set of incredible motherhood "Spidey-Senses," and it's about time we shut out the noise from outside and listen to our kick-ass inner-self. Trust her, she knows where it's at.

One of the most rewarding parts of my job is empowering a new mother to embrace her instincts. Every time I hear the sound of joy in a woman's voice when she's listened to her gut and "got it right," I rejoice for the sisterhood.

# BREASTFEEDING
## POSITIONS

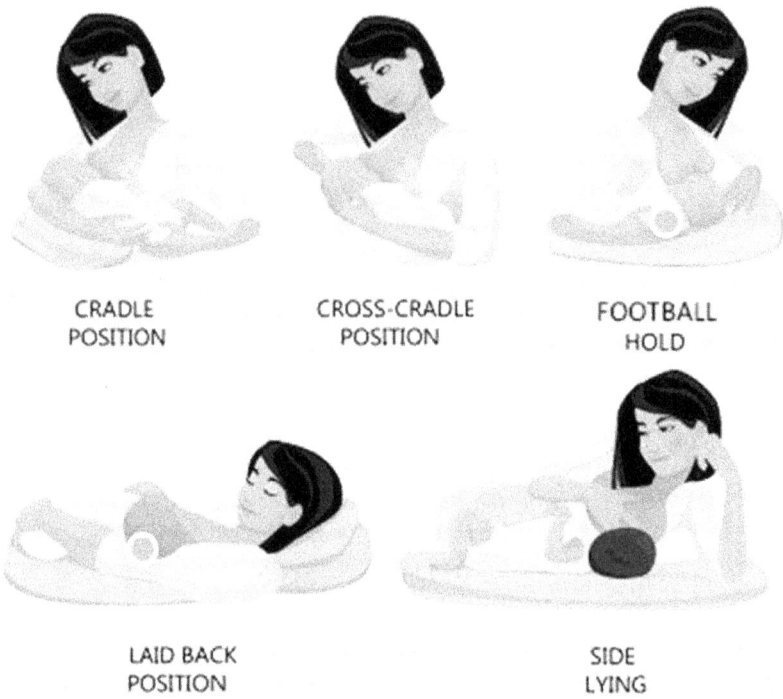

Now, it wouldn't be a complete chapter if I only explained one position to you and sent you on your merry way, so I have explained some others below, as well as how to perform them so the risk of injury to your boobs and back is reduced.

**Cradle Hold (Madonna Hold)**

The most popular position is the "Madonna" or "Cradle Hold." It feels the most natural to most mothers, yet is one of the most difficult in achieving a great latch. The hold, when performed improperly, is detrimental for ongoing support and care for a mother's anatomy (hunching over the baby for years does damage to your rotator cuffs – ask any osteo, physio or massage therapist – and requires, sitting which is difficult if you have had an episiotomy, Caesarean, or have haemorrhoids.

Of course, because it feels most natural to mothers, we instinctively use it again and again. So, let's learn how to do it properly, shall we?

Some pointers:

- Baby needs to lie across the mother's forearm on the side that the mother will be using for the feed.
- Baby's head is either in the bed of the elbow or midway down the forearm, which results in the best positioning of baby's mouth with the mother's nipple.
- The baby's lower arm can be placed around the mother's back or tucked down along next to his or her body.
- The baby's legs can be wrapped around the mother's waist, if needed to bring the baby closer to the breast.
- Baby's entire body should be facing the mother, chest to chest rather than chest to ceiling.
- Baby's mouth should be level with the mother's nipple, and a pillow is needed to support the baby's body in the mother's lap to ensure the baby is brought up to the breast. (Versus the mother leaning down to the baby, which is detrimental for the mother's back and may ensure a drag-down with the latch).
- A pillow is needed to support Mother's arm and back.

IMPORTANT NOTES ON THE MADONNA HOLD:

Many Mothers who have come to me have found that a few months into their breastfeeding journey, they can feel shooting pains in the front of their breasts whilst breastfeeding. After I've asked a few questions, I've found the problem to be that the breastfeeding mother is hunching forward. The solution? Get her to sit up straight!

The referred pain from a mother leaning forward for up to 8-12 times a day (which is the normal amount of breastfeeds in a zero- to -three-month-old baby) means that she will feel pains shooting down her breasts and which, over time, will give a mother severe shoulder pain. It's no wonder at this point many mothers give up breastfeeding altogether. Sitting up straight is *so* important, ladies, and pretty please, while we're at it, use supportive pillows for your good-self! Your back (and baby) can thank me later.

**Side Lying Position**

This is my all-time favourite position to use as a mother, especially when you've been breastfeeding for *dayyyyyyyys*! If you're experiencing fatigue or a forceful let down, it is the most popular position as well. This is because gravity is no longer your enemy – your breast is flat and not facing downwards towards the baby.

While the mother lies on her side, place a pillow behind her upper back, and have her roll backwards into the pillow so that the pillow stabilizes her. The baby is placed on the bed facing the mother (also on their side), with their nose in line with the nipple. This is so that when the baby puts their head back to feed, their neck is extended upwards, allowing the baby the opportunity to swallow and breathe. (Ever tried having a drink with your chin close to your chest? Pretty impossible, as we need to have our neck back to swallow.)

The mother then uses the arm on the side she is lying on to put the pillow under her head and the other arm, the one on top of her, is free to hold her baby. With the Mother's knees bent so her body is in a C-shape, it is impossible to roll onto your baby, and so is very safe. Recommended by the Australian Breastfeeding Association as a safe sleeping position, many mothers find that its quite simply the most joyful and relaxing way to feed their baby – especially when both fall asleep after a feed.

**Football Hold (Twin Hold)**

This position is, quite frankly, necessary if you are feeding twins, and many mothers of multiple births claim that its simply more efficient to feed both at once. Also, if you are needing to trial different positions other than the baby-led attachment or cradle hold, this one is useful for babies that have a preference to one side due to torticollis (neck twist – they must see an osteo or chiro to get this fixed), or due to Mum preferring a side. Yes, even mums have a "better side," and a weak left or right arm (due to a disability or injury) can mean that football hold can get a baby to attach to one side better than another position. There was a mother I counselled that had a weak left arm, for no other reason than she was a predominately right-handed lady, so she fed both her babies with a cradle hold on the right breast, and a football hold on the left.

There are no hard and fast rules as to which position you chose. It is an individual journey and one that only you and your baby can figure out. But there are road bumps to every journey, and they must be discussed if they seem abnormal.

A baby that prefers one breast over the other may need their neck looked at.

Post-birth, the first thing I recommend *all* mothers and babies do is to have at least one visit to the osteo, physio or chiro that deals with kids. Regardless of how natural it is to have a baby squished inside of us for nine months (well, its mainly the last trimester that does all the squishing), it's possible that your baby's neck and spine may need a gentle massage post birth. This gentle, non-invasive treatment can mean the difference between continuing to breastfeed, or not.

Fussing at the breast can mean a baby is in pain. Crying at the breast can mean a baby is in pain. Refusing the breast can mean a baby is in pain.

Please seek the right advice by consulting a qualified IBCLC lactation consultant (they must be IBCLC-qualified) and an osteopath, a chiropractor or a paediatric physiotherapist. NO. ONE. ELSE.

I am passionate about mothers receiving the *right* advice. When it comes to breastfeeding advice, please only contact an IBCLC Lactation Consultant. They are breastfeeding *experts* and have the skills and knowledge to help and refer you to the right expert for all your breastfeeding concerns.

## So *Why* Breastfeed?

My strongest belief, aside from the one that love conquers all, is that it is absolutely necessary to feed your baby human milk (breastfeed). As a lactation consultant, I have the honour of working with a group of people subject to one of the last widely accepted prejudices: feeding your baby from your body.

Some of these people have suffered a lot by the time they see me, such as physical pain due to poor positioning and attachment, cracked nipples, and a whole lot of confusion as to whether they should be feeding from the breast at all. Many mothers claim that the information regarding breastfeeding is so conflicting amongst health professionals, it has almost become a widespread mystery.

Yet there is one national authority on breastfeeding that can help, and whose information regarding teaching mothers to breastfeed isn't a secret at all: the Australian Breastfeeding Association (ABA).

This national organisation is the leading authority on breastfeeding in Australia. The information they provide is evidence-based knowledge derived from research from the World Health Organisation (WHO), and the breastfeeding counsellors – who are available to you, FOR FREE – have been trained in counselling and breastfeeding knowledge for a longer period of time than a doctor! These women, who volunteer eight hours per month for the admirable cause of breastfeeding, are experienced themselves in lactation. Lactation is very much like art: hard to control, somewhat messy, sometimes confusing, but intrinsically beautiful and a little left of centre.

These mums are trained to a national standard to give mums reassurance, evidence-based information, and referrals to other professions, all unique and dependent on the caller's situation. All of this is available for FREE to all mothers in Australia – in fact, if you become a member, you can receive monthly newsletters, and join your local group to connect with counsellors and breastfeeders in your community.

This is why breastfeeding is so very important:

- It contains antibodies to help protect your baby from the illnesses you are both exposed to.
- It provides a complete meal for your baby for the first six months of life.
- Breastmilk has just the right amount of "species-specific" protein, fats, salts, sugars and other nutrients for a baby's sensitive digestive system.
- It ensures your baby has a lower risk of allergies, gastrointestinal Illness, morbidity, SIDS, tooth decay, juvenile diabetes, colic, infectious disease, and childhood cancers.
- Formula INCREASES your risks of all of the above, particularly MORBIDITY.
- Breastfeeding lowers a mother's risk of breast and ovarian cancer and osteoporosis.
- There is no risk of contamination, because breastmilk is delivered straight from the breast to the baby.
- Breastfed babies have higher IQs and a stronger sense of emotional security because of their physical connection to their mother through breastfeeding.

- Women step into their roles as mothers faster because of the close contact with baby, and the fulfilling bonding qualities of breastfeeding.
- It is the cleanest food your child will EVER have. Environmentally and sustainably, there is no carbon footprint after a breastfeed.
- Breastfeeding not only saves human lives, but it saves energy, natural resources, and money – not just for the baby's family, but the whole world!

**What is in breastmilk?**

Immunoglobin A and immunoglobin G are the factors that boost the immune system, and which are essential for a growing baby's development.

The level of immunoglobulin A in breastmilk remains high from day 10 to at least seven and a half months post-partum. Human milk contains 0.8%-0.9% protein, 4.5% fat, 7.1% carbohydrates and 0.2% ash (minerals). Carbohydrates are mainly lactose, but the exact composition of breastmilk varies from day to day, depending on food consumption and environment (meaning that the ration of water to fat fluctuates).

COMPARISON TO OTHER MILKS

All mammalian species produce milk, but the composition of milk for each species varies widely, and other kinds of milk are often very different from human breastmilk. As a rule, the milk of mammals that nurse frequently (including human babies) is less rich, or more watery, than the milk of mammals whose young nurse less often. Human milk is noticeably thinner and sweeter than cow's milk, for example Whole cow's milk doesn't contain sufficient vitamin E or essential fatty acids, and it also contains excessive amounts of protein, sodium, and potassium, which may put a strain on an infant's immature kidneys (as discussed earlier). In addition, the proteins and fats in whole cow's milk are more difficult for an infant to digest and absorb than the ones in breastmilk. Evaporated milk may be easier to digest due to the processing of the protein, but it is still nutritionally inadequate.

## ALTERNATIVES USES FOR BREASTMILK OTHER THAN FEEDING

Does anyone know of any uses for breastmilk other than feeding a baby/toddler? You can use it as a home remedy for minor ailments such as conjunctivitis, insect bites and stings, and contact dermatitis, as well as infected wounds, burns, and abrasions. It can be used as a face cleanser, as well as eye-makeup remover, as contact lens solution, and even to boost the immune system of ill persons having viral gastroenteritis, influenza, the common cold, and pneumonia – all because of its immunologic properties.

Some medical experts are convinced that breastmilk can induce apoptosis in some types of cancer cells, however more research and evidence are needed in this area of cancer treatment.

There is a story about a young girl in Queensland with a life-threatening tumour whose mother asked for donations of EBM after reading about the benefits of breastmilk. She attended an ABA meeting at Maroochydore and mothers from the ABA donated milk by the gallon. The child made a significant turnaround and was able to attend school almost four months later after taking daily doses of breastmilk smoothies (about 500 millilitres a day).

There have been anecdotal reports of treating cancer with breastmilk, but no formal research has been undertaken, though in the laboratory it has been found something in breastmilk knocks off cancer cells. In America they have donor milk banks and you can get it with a prescription.

Some restaurateurs have used human breastmilk as a substitute for cow's milk in dairy products and food recipes, and there is a book titled *A Breastfeeding Mother's Secret Recipes*, providing a lengthy compilation of detailed food and beverage recipes containing human breastmilk.

Attempts to formulate soap from breastmilk have also been made, and those using it claim that its effectiveness as a cleanser is greater than or equal to, that of traditional soaps.

Finally, the most amazing thing that is in breastmilk is its uniqueness and individuality to suit the child it is producing for. No one person is alike, which is the same to be said for the breastmilk being provided for each baby!

The immune function of breastmilk is individual, as the mother, through her touching and taking care of the baby, comes into contact with pathogens that colonize on the baby, and, as a consequence, her body makes the appropriate antibodies and immune cells. This basically means that if you are taking your breastfed child to day care, it is worth staying in that environment for a while so that your body soaks up the "germs" in order for your body to produce the antibodies for your child and protect them with your next breastfeed – amazing!

Learning to breastfeed is a two-way street; both baby and Mum need to learn how to do this together. Even if your birth hasn't ended up the way you planned, simply attaching the baby to your nipple as soon as medically possible will be the way it all begins. And as discussed, the best position for breastfeeding is baby-led attachment – let your baby find its way to the breast and "crawl" onto your nipple is as nature intended. It's a beautiful process to watch nature in action, but it is also important to support the baby from falling off of Mum's chest and gently guiding them as they make their way to the nipple for their first feed.

The key to a great breastfeed is positioning and attachment. Bring your baby "up" to you, and have them chest to chest, and chin to breast. Their lips should be flanged, and you shouldn't hear any clicking noises, which could indicate a break in the seal. The baby needs to have a strong suck on the breast – remember, it's breastfeeding, NOT nipple feeding. If the baby is attached incorrectly, please don't sit through the pain. It will only damage your nipples, and a damaged nipple is just like any other injury of the body and can become infected.

When you position your baby, you need to aim the nipple at the baby's nose and, when their mouth opens wide, flick it into the back of their mouth so that the nipple is sitting at the back of their mouth, not rubbing on the roof of their palate. Otherwise, that will be the cause of cracked nipples, which is something all new mothers should expect! You didn't learn to drive without swerving a few times, so please remember: this is a learning *journey*, not a race.

Please note: if you do get cracked nipples, please just express a little breastmilk on the cracks and blow dry – the anti-bacterial qualities in breastmilk are amazing, and will heal all wounds.(I have, while lactating, squirted some on even my own cuts and scrapes. I promise you; it heals a wound faster and more naturally than any synthetic product – it's simply liquid gold!

Also, please keep in mind that poor positioning and attachment can lead to blocked ducts, which can also lead to mastitis or an abscess. If you feel like your breast is hot and hard, don't panic. Try to gently (and I mean gently) massage the lump out towards the nipple. If your milk is sitting in your breasts, and is not being drained by the baby, it can eventually leak into the interstitial breast tissue. Our ducts are permeable, which means that you will have breastmilk where it shouldn't be.

Ensure that your breasts are fully drained in the first two to four weeks of breastfeeding ensures that you will establish a milk supply this is important! If you do not establish that milk supply, then you are looking at an uphill battle for the rest of your journey. Too many people are afraid of engorgement at this stage, and yet it's absolutely imperative that you fully drain the breasts so that you begin the milk making loop. You should drain the breasts (both of them) every two to three hours, for two to four weeks. If your baby is only taking one side, then express the other side. And then once your supply is established, you can go to block feeding.

Sleepiness is common in the first couple of weeks post birth.

Undressing the baby, and feeding skin-to-skin (to elicit oxytocin in both Mum and baby), will help to keep baby awake. Tickle your baby's toes and so on, to try to keep the baby awake, giving them the opportunity to have the best feed possible.

Feed frequently if you have to. Its normal to feed eight to 12 times in a 24-hour period. Don't look at the clock! The only number you need to look at is how many wet nappies they have had. What goes in, must come out. More than 6 heavy wet nappies? That is a healthy, well-fed baby.

If your baby has good skin tone, is generally happy between feeds, has more than six nappies, regular stools, and can settle easily, then they are getting enough. Don't worry about how long your baby takes to feed; how long your baby takes to feed will be how long *they* take!

Want to know how to treat your baby? Respect your baby's individuality from birth regarding everything they do, is like receiving their manual – listen to them. Every new soul is born with their own individual way of eating, so respect their ways and you will have a very happy baby.

Think about it: how do *you* eat? Are you a grazer? Do you have a solid three meals a day? Or do you only eat one meal a day? Do you eat fast or slow? How do *you* need to be treated? Uniquely! We are individually and perfectly made by our Creator, and we each have our own purpose here on Earth.

Imagine if we felt safe loved and respected from birth – that would surely result in an emotionally-stable, well-nourished and self confident-person right there.

# Chapter 3.

# THE MINDFUL MOTHER (BREASTFEEDING MEDITATIONS)

When I became a mother and a counsellor, I developed strategies for myself that "worked" for other mothers. I share these secret strategies with you now. They have been a gift to me my rise to become the mother I was meant to be.

This is key: everyone is unique, and everyone has their own soul journey to take. The empowerment right now is that you recognise your own ability to rise into the shoes you create yourself as a parent, not somebody else's.

My absolute secret to breastfeeding success is understanding the "let down." The let down is where the baby triggers the nerves in your nipples to turn on prolactin, the milk-making hormone, and oxytocin, the love hormone. Oxytocin here is key – once it is triggered, it ejects milk from the breasts – without it, your milk will not come out.

The three reasons why Oxytocin will be inhibited are stress, exhaustion, and illness, so when mothers ring me and tell me their milk has "dried up," I ask them if they are experiencing any of the above . It is a yes, every single time.

It is actually biologically impossible for milk to dry up. So please be reassured that this doesn't just "happen over night. And if you wake up one morning and swear it's gone, I promise you, its just as readily available to you as learning the Let Down Meditation I created and have used, not just myself but for thousands of mothers over the last decade.

The let down is an interesting and very clever reflex. It is internally- (by feeling love, having the nerve endings on your nipples stimulated, and by thinking loving thoughts) and externally- (by hearing the baby cry, being stressed out by an external factor) triggered.

The beautiful thing about it is that it makes it possible for you to turn it around in one meditation. The power of a positive thought outweighs 50 negative thoughts!

So here you are, stressed, tired, and feeling like absolute shit. Your baby is nine months old and you've been getting up three to six hours of sleep a night for the whole time. Then a partner or family member weighs in on your situation and/or you have an illness that is out of your control. Your milk supply gets lower and lower, bringing you more and more stress. You try to express (by this stage, unless you have been expressing regularly and understand how to trigger oxytocin when expressing) and you feel like a cow and decide that your milk has gone and you feel pressure to "give up breastfeeding."

This situation is one faced by 80% of the mothers that I have dealt with over the years, including my own. This situation is able to be overturned. Here's what you do:

First, go buy a galactagogue (a supplement that increases milk supply) such as fenugreek, the *only* galactagogue that I recommend. Next, grab yourself the "Magic Beans" (fruit, vegetable, and berries JuicePlus capsules), plus the vegan protein powders (also safe for children) – you absolutely *need* to be refuelling yourself nutritionally, and they are the only ones I recommend to be safe whilst pregnant or lactating. I have provided information at the end of the book to show how to get your hands on these micronutrients.

Lastly, use my let down meditation and learn it. This meditation, once practiced, will work at any time you aren't feeling like your let down is not immediately responding. When you've been exhausted, your brain/body connection is somewhat discordant. As you are now in a "mother-fog" all of the time, the neurons have stopped talking to each other. By simply reciting the words in my meditation, you will start to fire off the neurons, and create new pathways for this incredible hormone, oxytocin, to be fired off whenever you need it.

## The Let Down Meditation:

This meditation is designed to teach your Body how to LetDown.
*The number one reason why your LetDown won't happen is Stress.*
*The number one solution for dealing with stress is meditation.*

The LetDown Reflex is necessary for milk supply because the more Milk you remove from your Breasts, the more milk your body makes.
Let us Begin.

Sit up straight
Close your eyes,
Slowly Take a breath and Inhale through your nose **(inhale)**
and Exhale through your mouth **(exhale)**
....and Relax.
Feel your body relax.
Again inhale through your Nose, **(inhale)**
Hold it.
And as you Exhale, **(exhale)**
Relax.
And one more Slow, steady breath through your nose. **(inhale)**
And as you exhale, **(exhale)**
Feel your body deeply relax.

I want you to picture your baby,
Feel the Love in your Heart as you think about your baby.
Feel that Love move through your entire body.
From your head down to your toes,
You feel Love, you ARE Love.

Now, Breath IN deeply, (inhale)
and on the exhale say to yourself, "Let Down" "Let Down"

Breath In (inhale)
and exhale „Let Down" „Let Down"

Breath In (inhale)

and exhale „Let Down" „Let Down"

Now While you are breathing in and out, telling yourself to Let Down on every exhale, I want you to visualise a Jug.
In your mind see a Large jug that is filled with your breastmilk.
Now visualise that jug tipping out your breastmilk.
You can see your milk pouring out of the jug.

Breath In (inhale)
and exhale „Let Down" „Let Down"

Breath In (inhale)
and exhale „Let Down" „Let Down"

Breath In (inhale)
and exhale „Let Down" „Let Down"

Visualise that jug again and again, know that it is filled with YOUR milk, and every time you see it your body remembers to "Let Down" "Let Down".

Breath In (inhale)
and exhale „Let Down" „Let Down"

Breath In (inhale)
and exhale „Let Down" „Let Down"

Breath In (inhale)
and exhale „Let Down" „Let Down"

Feel the connection with your baby,
Feel how much you love your beautiful baby,
Feel the joy and bond with your new baby.

Deeply connected.
Deeply bonded.
Deeply in love with your baby.

Breath in (inhale)
and exhale, "Let Down, "Let Down".

Breath In (inhale)
and exhale „Let Down" „Let Down"

Breath In (inhale)
and exhale „Let Down" „Let Down"

As the feed continues, keep breathing in and exhaling the words
"Let Down Let Down."
Continue to visualise your jug, filled with **your** breastmilk,
pouring out an abundant supply of milk, for your beautiful baby.
Thank you for breastfeeding your baby, you are saving the world, one breastfed baby at a time.

### The Expressing Let Down Meditation:

This meditation is designed to teach your Body how to LetDown when expressing.

*The number one reason why your LetDown won't happen is Stress.*

*The number one solution for dealing with stress is meditation*

The LetDown Reflex is necessary for milk supply, because the more milk you remove from your Breast, the more milk you body makes.
If you are feeling stressed, ill or exhausted, this can affect you from having a LetDown which, eventually, affects your milk supply.

This meditation is especially necessary for tired, stressed and exhausted Mothers, and with practice, has Proven to help you trigger the LetDown reflex in seconds just by using the Visualisation and Breathing tools I am about to teach you.

You can do this Meditation with, or without, your Breast Pump attached.
Let us Begin.

Sit up straight
Close your eyes
Slowly Take a breath and Inhale through your nose **(inhale)**
and Exhale through your mouth **(exhale)**
....and Relax.
Feel your body relax.
Again inhale through your Nose **(inhale),**
Hold it.
And as you Exhale **(exhale)**,
Relax.
And one more Slow, steady breath through your nose.
**(inhale)**
And as you exhale, **(exhale)**
Feel your body deeply relax.

I want you to picture your baby,
Feel the Love in your Heart as you think about your baby.
Feel that Love move through your entire body.
From your head down to your toes,
You feel Love, you **are** Love.

Now, Breath IN deeply through your nose (inhale)

and as you exhale say to yourself, "Let Down" "Let Down"

Breath In (inhale)
and exhale „Let Down" „Let Down"

Breath In (inhale)
and exhale „Let Down" „Let Down"

The power of your mind can release Oxytocin, the Love Hormone.
This hormone will trigger the let down reflex, which will help to increase your milk supply.
Continue to take deep breaths through your nose, (inhale)
and Exhale through your mouth.
„Let Down" „Let Down"

Now I want you to visualise a Jug.
In your mind picture a Large jug that is filled with your breastmilk.
Now visualise that jug tipping out your breastmilk.
You can see your milk pouring out of the jug.

Breath In (inhale)
and exhale
„Let Down" „Let Down"

Think again about your baby,
This will bring on all the infinite Love you have
for your new child. Love with trigger the LetDown reflex.

Breath In (inhale)
and exhale „Let Down" „Let Down"

Breath In (inhale)
and exhale „Let Down"  „Let Down"

As you express remember what you are doing for your baby.
You are doing the best thing for your baby by feeding it breastmilk, which is laying strong foundations of your babys immune system.
Literally nothing else on earth can do this for Your baby Except Breastmilk.
And no one else has your milk.
Your Milk is designed for Your baby.
And Only You can Express Milk to Nourish and Sustain Your baby.

Breath In (inhale)
and exhale  „Let Down"  „Let Down"

Breath In (inhale)
and exhale  „Let Down"  „Let Down"

Breath In (inhale)
and exhale  „Let Down"  „Let Down"

You are doing a wonderful Job.
Continue to Express until the milk slows to a trickle.
Don't watch the clock.
Every Mother's Milk flows at different speeds and volumes, please listen to your body and respect its individual capabilities.
Your Milk is enough for Your baby.

Breath In (inhale)
and exhale  „Let Down"  „Let Down"

Breath In (inhale)
and exhale „Let Down" „Let Down"

Breath In (inhale)
and exhale „Let Down" „Let Down"

As the music continues, keep breathing in and exhaling
"Let Down Let Down".
Continue to picture your jug, filled with your breastmilk, pouring out an abundant supply of milk, for your beautiful baby.
Thank you for feeding your baby breastmilk, you are saving the world, one breastfed baby at a time.

# Chapter 4.

# PREPARING FOR YOUR RISE (SOUL WORK FOR MOTHERS AND PARTNERS)

> *Children will often act out something they have seen or heard, and their power of imitation astounds adults. According to Rudolph Steiner, the child's whole inner urge is to be "alike," to be at one with the environment, thus they need to be surrounded by adults whose actions (and feelings and thoughts) are worthy of imitation.*

When you become a mother or father, something wonderful inside of you comes alive – it is the archetypal Wild Woman (or Alpha Male) that leaps through your blood and howls at the moon as you are putting your baby to your breast or chest. A doctor who was helping me throughout my first year as a mum once told me that if you poured boiling water over a mother's arm whilst she is holding her newborn baby, she will not drop it – that's how strong her instincts for her baby are. I resonated so much with that concept, and simply vibrated with a new sense of purpose on this Earth: the purpose of a mother.

One of the most important things you can do to prepare as a mother is to set yourself onto the path of your *own* motherhood journey, a path that is uniquely yours and yours alone – met and only paralleled by the baby's other parent. It is imperative that you discover who you are as a mother so that you are not triggered by your baby due to your own upbringing.

This is even true if you had the most wonderful upbringing of them all and your family is classed as close and "normal." It is still important to tread your own soul's path as a mother, because you are not your mother and your baby is not you. If you don't do this work, you will be triggered with feelings of anger, sadness or trauma. You may feel yourself overwhelmed instead of empathetic to a crying baby and that can sometimes lead to being traumatised – that is a very unhealthy environment for a baby to be raised in.

If you don't do the soul work and tread your own path, one day the past may trip you up and haunt you in the way of triggers, traumas, or a long-lost child, fed up with the family cycle of destruction that you are unwittingly passing on to yet another generation. Authenticity is truth, and children are the best BS detectors on Earth, so if you are treading someone else's path, they may smell a rat. Soul work is as important as eating, and discovering who you are as a mother or father is as equally important, before or immediately after, baby arrives.

> *The child's future later depends on those who influenced the earliest years. - Rudolf Steiner*

Once I became a parent, I became a lot of things, and I also *un*-became a lot of things. But what I did know? And that became Glaringly obvious once I pushed a human being out of my body? I hadn't prepared for this baby properly.

I mean, sure I had the cot, the clothes, and the nappies, but I hadn't really felt into what this was going to mean for me and my partner after the baby was born, let alone, what kind of a life I was going to be able to provide for this new soul. And when baby came; I came apart. However, I did know one thing – and one thing only: I HAD to get my shit together. Fast. The process of sorting your shit out is not easy. It is for the keen, adventurous and brave. As a parent, you are on the frontlines of raising the new generation on Earth, and you are responsible for raising a species of kind and loving human beings, one "emotionally-adjusted" child at a time. Nothing else matters. *Be the change you want to see in the world.*

The "root" of all of the emotional problems in our adult lives begins with our childhood not giving us the emotional stability we need. Through intentional and unintentional interactions with the mother and father figures in our lives, we have developed resentments around certain interactions, and it's important to learn to heal the past in order to enjoy the present.

This even includes deep trauma, neglect, and abuse. True healing is available to you nowadays, and this inner child process works effectively and is everlasting. If you have the courage to pursue the road of self-sovereignty, then you will be rewarded with a life of self-love, radical self-acceptance, and an independence that absolutely nobody can take away from you. Our inner child is within all of us still, resisting, and sometimes cowering in fear, when our current adult situations trigger emotions from our childhood. When this happens, it can be a grateful "note to self" that our healing journey needs some "attending to" – the key is in honouring our Inner child.

**The Workshops:**

**Step 1: Inner Child Work:** bringing your inner child home.

When your baby is born, you are born again. For some people this is uncomfortable, and they struggle. For others, it can be a great experience, an opportunity as it were, to re-birth themselves into a new life and new purpose as a parent. In fact, many people flourish with this re-birthing. When you give birth to your baby, it can be as if you simultaneously give birth to your inner child.

Be very careful, however, to recognize that your newborn baby is separate from you. You need to raise your "child" alongside your inner child.

Also, you also risk losing yourself completely in your actual child, living through them, and turning them into your inner child, thus blurring the lines between them and you. This will prevent them from standing in their own truth and being their own individual person, which will, in turn, perhaps make them resent you. And you will resent them for not becoming who YOU wanted them to be. So therefore, you risk losing them, and of course, losing yourself.

Write down your childhood traumas, writing down three things you remember from each age bracket. (It's fine, however, if you only remember one or two, or none at all).

For the purpose of the meditation, think of the most prominent moments that you believe brought you the most pain. Whether they made you feel angry, sad, or in pain, these are the moments that you need to heal.

Now, before the meditation, think of the bedroom you had from one of those ages (if you were like me and moved around a lot, think of the bedroom from the time you are willing to re-explore and to heal). You need to have this visual in your head, ready to meet yourself at those moments in your childhood. Remember to continue to do this meditation until all the "stuff" has been cleared, and you are at peace and completely whole with your inner child.

Some people may need to only do this once, others need to do it multiple times. It doesn't matter, as long as you do it, and get your "shit" sorted.

**Inner Child Meditation:**

*"Bring your Inner child back home with you and heal old wounds"*

Let us Heal past wounds for your Inner child and then bring them home with you, to be with you as an adult, so that you can parent your child and honour them as the individual soul that they are. Thus avoiding parenting your inner child instead of your actual child.

Let us begin.

Sit up straight
Close your eyes
Slowly Take a breath and Inhale through your nose **(inhale)**
and Exhale **(exhale)**
....and Relax.
Feel your body relax.
Again inhale through your Nose, **(inhale)**
Hold it.
And as you Exhale, **(exhale)**
Relax.
And one more Slow, steady breath through your nose. **(inhale)**
And as you exhale, **(exhale)**
Feel your body relax.

I want you to Visualise yourself walking into the childhood bedroom you had at any age.
I want you to walk over to your child self,
Sit down beside your inner child and face yourself.
Look deep into your child's eyes.
What did you look like?
Really take in your child self and as you look into your child's eyes.
I want you to give that child all your Love.

Now lean over and give your child self a big hug.
Now, without letting go,
I want you to whisper in your child's ear,
Tell your inner child that you didn't deserve to feel or experience any of those sad, confusing or fearful moments from your childhood.

Tell yourself, "Children shouldn't feel that much fear."

"You didn't deserve to feel like you had done something wrong."
"It wasn't your responsibility. Children shouldn't be afraid."
"Children are meant to feel safe, loved and respected."
Tell your child self whatever else you feel you need to say right now.

Hold your inner child's hand.
Look into your inner child's eyes.
And send more love into your very own soul.
Now say to your inner child, "Everything is going to be ok,"
Say it again, "Everything is going to be OK"
Say to them, "I promise you, you are now safe and now that I'm here, I'm never letting you go"
Explain to them again that you are grown up now and that you are OK.
Tell them that they are coming home with you, and they are
Safe now and everything is going to be OK.

Now stand up, take your inner child by the hand, and as you walk out of the bedroom know that you are bringing your inner child home with you.

Now breath in Through your nose (**inhale**)
And exhale through your mouth (**exhale**)

Realise how brave you are that you have shown
Deep Love and Grace For Yourself.
You are demonstrating Love by going back for your Inner Child.
You are Healing the Past and have brought your Inner child home with you into your present

You are nurturing your inner child in a way no one else could,
And by you parenting yourself, you show deep personal respect.
Your radical self reliance begins today.
You and your inner child will now forever be as one.

Sit with these feelings.
Put your hand on your heart and feel your inner child in there.
Feel them thank you for coming to get them.
Let yourself cry.
Let yourself laugh.
Release and Let yourself go through all emotions.
Process those feelings, accept them and try to move forward.

Now, slowly bring yourself back to your body.
And Remember who you have with you now.
Your Inner Child.
You are now ready to face the World,
Inner child and Adult you,.
Together as one.
Repeat this meditation as often as you need, when and if your past memories haunt your inner child and they need you to step in for them and bring them back home again.

Sit back and listen to the music while you integrate this healing and self nurturing experience.

**Step 2 - The Internal Parent Work** (What type of parent do you want to be?)

When you become a parent, the sum of all of the parents who raised you becomes your "internal parent." Discovering your "internal mother" or "internal father" is one of the most important things you can do, aside from taking care of that beautiful amazing new baby you just had (or are about to have).

First, you must recognize who that internal parent is. Write down who your mother and father are, as well as the other mother or father figures in your life from your childhood (this can include aunts, uncles, grandparents and so on.)Now write down all the prominent and memorable characteristics of these people (e.g., kind, passive-aggressive, angry, assertive, distant, emotionally intelligent).

Separate them into "Embrace" versus "Release."

Now look for the internal parent traits you want to embrace. Honour these traits and cherish them as ones you *want* to Identify with as a parent. For the traits that you *want to release*, acknowledge, first and foremost, that they are traits of the internal parent that are not. Recognise that it was a part of your make up as a parent, but it is not your *identity*. Once you lose yourself to that internal parent, you become your past, and the sum of all of the parents that raised you. You risk becoming a child again.

Now, after writing down the internal parent traits you want to embrace, you need to remove those that you do not. Here's the meditation to release all the traits you want to remove from your life.

**Parent Cleanse Meditation:**

This meditation is designed to help you cleanse the three main negative traits from your parents or significant adults who influenced you during your childhood.

When you become a Parent, the sum of all parents who raised you become your "Internal Parent".
Once you have recognized who that Internal Parent is; we can cleanse the traits that you don't want to keep from the influences you have had in your life.
Because if you lose connection with the essence of yourself to the Internal Parent, you then risk behaving like them towards your child. For the memories may trigger you and you may begin parenting from a place of Fear.
Thereby increasing your chance of experiencing triggers when YOUR Child starts to behave in ways similar to YOU in your childhood.

Let the cleanse begin.

Sit up straight
close your eyes
Slowly Take a breath and Inhale **(inhale)**
and Exhale **(exhale)**
....and Relax.
Feel your body relax.
Again inhale through your Nose, **(inhale)**
Hold it.
And as you Exhale, **(inhale)**
Relax.
And one more Slow, steady breath through your nose. **(inhale)**
And as you exhale, (**inhale**)
Feel your body relax.

And now, become aware of the Infinite Parents you have inside of you.
These are all the Women and Men who have influenced you as you grew up.

Think about your Mother, your Aunts, Your Grandmother.
What is the Legacy they have left for you?
This is your Internal Mother.
Think about your own Father, your Uncle, Your Grandfather.
What is the Legacy they have left for you?
This is your Internal Father.

Together they make up Your Internal Parent.
This Internal Parent represents the
Good Parent and the Bad Parent.

It's important to see who this Internal Parent is.
To acknowledge their condition within you as you are, right now.
We are going to cleanse yourself of anything that no longer serves you.
We need to do this, so that you are not triggered by your child.

So now,
I want you to think about the first negative trait that you felt didn't serve you as a child
Think of the actions of the parents you had, what did they do?
How did this make you feel?
I want you to feel this emotionally.
Bring it all to the surface now.
"it's OK, you are safe."
Feel the emotion this trait made you feel.
Let it embody you.
Where can you feel this?
In your head?
In your tummy?
In your heart?

Feel the emotion and let it take over your body.
"It's ok, You are safe."

Become aware of this emotion in your body and bring yourself back to the present,
And realise that you are OK.
You are an adult now and can feel this emotion within you,
yet you still know that you are ok.
This emotion can no longer control you.
it belongs to the parents of your past.
To leave it in the past we Must move through it
and then send them away with breath and let it GO.

Take a deep breath in (**inhale**)
and as you exhale
Let GO....Let GO.

breath in (**inhale**)
and as you exhale
Let GO....Let GO.

last one
breath in (**inhale**)
and as you exhale
Let GO....Let GO.

I want you to think about the second negative trait that you felt didn't serve you as a child
Think of the actions of the parents you had, what did they do?
How did this make you feel?
I want you to feel this emotionally. Bring it all to the surface now.
"it's OK, you are safe."
Feel the emotion this trait made you feel.

Let it embody you.
Where can you feel this?
In your head?
In your tummy?
In your heart?
Feel the emotion and let it take over your body.
"It's ok, You are safe."

Become aware of this emotion in your body and bring yourself back to the present,
And realise that you are OK.
You are an adult now and can feel this emotion within you,
yet you still know that you are ok.
This emotion can no longer control you.
it belongs to the parents of your past.
To leave it in the past we Must move through it
and then send it away with breath and let it GO.

Take a deep breath in (**inhale**)
and as you exhale
Let GO....Let GO.

breath in (**inhale**)
and as you exhale
Let GO....Let GO.

last one
breath in (**inhale**)
and as you exhale
Let GO....Let GO.

I want you to think about the third negative trait that you felt didn't serve you as a child
Think of the actions of the parents you had, what did they do?

How did this make you feel?
I want you to feel this emotionally. Bring it all to the surface now.
"it's OK, you are safe."
Feel the emotion this trait made you feel.
Let it embody you.
Where can you feel this?
In your head?
In your tummy?
In your heart?
Feel the emotion and let it take over your body.
"It's ok, You are safe."

Become aware of this emotion in your body and bring yourself back to the present,
And realise that you are OK.
You are an adult now and can feel this emotion within you,
yet you still know that you are ok.
This emotion can no longer control you.
it belongs to the parents of your past.
To leave it in the past we Must move through it
and then send it away with breath and let it GO.

Take a deep breath in (**inhale**)
and as you exhale
Let GO....Let GO.

breath in (**inhale**)
and as you exhale
Let GO....Let GO.
last one
breath in (**inhale**)
and as you exhale
Let GO....Let GO.

Now I want you to embody yourself with LOVE.
Feel your heart open up towards yourself,
Love yourself as much as you can!
Enjoy feeling this Love within your entire body,
Love is the great Healer and
you can nurture yourself into life.

Now say to your Internal Parent, "Everything is going to be ok,"
Say to yourself, "I am the Parent now, This is MY Journey"

You are Safe, Loved and Respected
If you feel the emotions those negative traits made you feel again, this is what you say
"Thank you for reminding me of how my parents made me feel.
this is not how I parent, I am who I say I am."

Today, You've Honoured yourself deeply,
You've acknowledged and released the traits that harmed you as a child.
You are breaking the family cycle and stepping into the Parent that You want to Be.
Remember, YOU say who you are as a Parent.

You are demonstrating Love by Honouring yourself as a Parent and respecting your child by healing the past.
You are Parenting yourself now.
Sit with the feelings.
Let yourself cry.
Let yourself laugh.
Let yourself be FREE.

Place your hand on your heart,
And Remember the honour you have showed yourself.
You say who you are.

Repeat this meditation as often as you so you can parent your child YOUR way.

If you need help "rising" to become the mother or father you say you are, and that God has planned you to be, I have two meditations that can assist you:

**The Mother Identity meditation:**

This meditation will help you learn to rise into your new identity and purpose as a Mother, to stand tall and be the Mother YOU want to be.

Let us Begin.

Sit up straight
Eyes closed
Slowly Take a breath and Inhale **(inhale)**
and Exhale **(exhale)**
....and Relax.
Feel your body relax.
Again inhale through your Nose, **(inhale)**
Hold it.
And as you Exhale, **(exhale)**
Relax.
And one more Slow, steady breath through your nose. **(inhale)**
And as you exhale, **(exhale)**
Feel your body relax.

And now, become aware of the Infinite Mothers you have inside of you.

These are all the Women who have influenced you as you grew up.
Think about your own Mother, Mothers of your friends, your Aunts, school teachers, even sports hero's.
What is the Legacy they left for you?
(pause)
That legacy is your Internal Mother.
She is made from the experience of not just your Mother, but of all
Mothering figures in your life.
Your Internal Mother represents the images of the Good Mother and the Bad Mother.

It's important to recognize this Internal Mother.
To acknowledge her condition within you as you are right now, as an Adult.
We must now dismantle the legacy that you have been left with.
Whatever traits you don't want, we are going to let them go, right now.

Take a deep breath in and pause.
As you exhale, let GO of the Mother figures that didn't serve you in your childhood.
(**exhale**).
Breath in (**inhale**)
and exhale (**exhale**)
Let GO, Let GO.

Some Mothers are women who have been taught to put culture and society above their children.
Some Mother still act out the fears of centuries of women before them, to try to mould their children so that they are accepted by their Culture and society.
This will divide a Mother and Child.

This will create Fear.
This fear doesn't need to belong to you now.
Seek YOUR Journey of Motherhood and assert your right to do this today.

Take a deep breath in and pause.
Then exhale.
Let Go, Let GO.

Stand in your truth now and say after me.

I am Safe.
I am Respected.
I am a Mother.

You have the power of your mind to bring forward your new Mother Identity.
Be The Mother that YOU want to be.

Even if you had the most wonderful Mother in the world, or None at all,
This one that we have created today.
Is You.
Engage with the Legacy of your Internal Mothers that only YOU want to keep.
You are doing the best you can.
You can do a Wonderful Job.

Please remember that Self Love takes practice.
Learn to Mother with Love and Mother with Courage and Joy.
Continue to listen to this to Integrate your new Mother identity.
Be Kind to yourself in your Journey as Mother.

**The Father Identity Meditation:**

This meditation will help you learn to rise into your new identity and purpose as a Father.

Sit up straight
Eyes closed
Slowly Take a breath and Inhale **(inhale)**
and Exhale **(exhale)**
....and Relax.
Feel your body relax.
Again inhale through your Nose, **(inhale)**
Hold it.
And as you Exhale, **(exhale)**
Relax.
And one more Slow, steady breath through your nose. **(inhale)**
And as you exhale, **(exhale)**
Feel your body relax.

And now, become aware of the Infinite Fathers you have inside of you.
These are all the Men who have influenced you as you grew up.
Think about your own Father, Fathers of your friends, your Uncles, school teachers, even sports hero's.
What is the Legacy they left for you?
(pause)
That legacy is your Internal Father.
He is made from the experience of not just your Father, but of all
Fathering figures in your life.
Your Internal Father represents the images of the Good Father and the Bad Father.

It's important to recognize this Internal Father.

To acknowledge his condition within you as you are right now, as an Adult.
We must now dismantle the legacy that you have been left with.
Whatever traits you don't want, we are going to let them go, right now.

Take a deep breath in and pause.
As you exhale, let GO of the father figures that didn't serve you in your childhood.
(**exhale**).
Breath in (**inhale**)
and exhale (**exhale**)
Let GO, Let GO.

Some Fathers are men who have been taught to put culture and society above their children.
Some Fathers still act out the fears of centuries of men before them, to try to mould their children so that they are accepted by their Culture and society.
This will divide a Father and Child.
This will create Fear.
This fear doesn't need to belong to you now.
Seek YOUR Journey of Fatherhood and assert your right to do this today.

Take a deep breath in and pause.
Then exhale.
Let Go, Let GO.

Stand in your truth now and say after me.

I am Safe.
I am Respected.
I am a Father.

You have the power of your mind to bring forward your new father
Identity.
Be The Father that YOU want to be.

Even if you had the most wonderful Father in the world, or None at all,
This one that we have created today.
Is You.
Engage with the Legacy of your Internal Fathers that only YOU want to keep.
You are doing the best you can.
You can do a Wonderful Job.

Please remember that Self Love takes practice.
Learn to Father with Love and Father with Courage and Joy.
Continue to listen to this to Integrate your new Father identity.
Be Kind to yourself in your Journey as Father.

**Step 3 - Triggers** (Your internal parent steps up)

A trigger is commonly known to be the part of a gun whereby if it is pulled back, the gun is now ready to fire. It is also a common term applied to a strong emotional reaction to another person. In this book, we will deal with that person being your own parent, but once you become a parent, commonly your own child will become the trigger. Shooting that "gun" at either party equals disaster, and even if you are the one to eventually apologise, the damage will already be done – and the wounds are often deep.

You know this, because you have them yourself. Someone fired the gun of life at you when you were a child, and regardless of how it was handled, it left marks. These scars became your own triggers.

If you don't deal with your inner child as per step one, or identify with your internal parent in step two, then the cycle will continue for future generations. Parents unable to step into their own identity as a parent often become a child themselves. When a trigger takes hold, they may possibly neglect the needs of their own child when the child acts a certain way, turning into the parental figure that fired the gun of life.

Here is a *really* simple way to stop losing your "stuff" and start parenting with a clear mind and a bucketload of empathy and emotional security.

*If you are triggered by your parent:*

This is very common. Why? Well we are only now in the age of consciousness , which is thankfully spreading very fast. The generations that raised us don't need to apologise; *we* need to cut the ties of the past and move forward, reclaiming our own identity in our lives as adults. Even if you had the most wonderful parents in the world, or none at all, a father or mother "figure" has shot the gun of life at you and has left a scar.

In your adult life, when you have a conversation with your parent and you are left feeling triggered, then identifying *exactly* how and why you are feeling that way is important. Pushing it down is not the answer; working through the trigger is imperative to your physical and emotional body. Remember that his or her (your parent's) reactions are a product of their life experiences and that their reactions are not yours. Thank them for the gift to heal and change.

Have you heard about the man that died of his heart hardening because he hardened his heart to life? This is not a joke or a myth – science proves that resentment is particularly bad for the cardiovascular system, and dealing with a trigger is important to your overall health and wellbeing. Make it a big a part of your daily exercises to remove resentment, for your heart's sake.

Identify that you have a trigger, and then identify what that trigger is. Let's say for example, your mother didn't reassure you, or liked to sit on the fence and not "take sides." This could make you feel unheard, unloved, and unbelieved. *Why can't she just take a stand and take my side for once?* your inner child may be grumbling. You may not say anything to your her, or maybe you do, but either way, she will not budge and refuses to be caught up in the scenario, thereby insisting her dogma of being a "diplomat" is important to her.

Once away from your parent, you can do this small exercise for yourself. Remember, you have the skills to support yourself. Sit quietly and slow your breath... and begin to parent yourself. Tell yourself everything you know to be your truth regarding the scenario. Say to yourself, *I believe you, I hear you, I am here for you, I have your back.* This is you parenting yourself, stepping into your ability to nurture yourself. Your mother and father may never change – in fact, I guarantee they will not. You don't need to make your parents see your side at all. The conversation is left in the past, but the outcome changes. Instead of feeling triggered – unheard (which you have probably felt all your life, these are *your* values versus *theirs,* remember?) or unappreciated – then you feel the triggers dissipate.

Why? Because you have suddenly developed the ability to have your own back. Have an "out loud" conversation with yourself; tell yourself out loud everything you need to hear in response to the situation you have just spoken to your parents about.

I promise you; the results are astonishing. Suddenly you don't need to bounce ideas off of anyone anymore. You have your own back, and the freedom from the dogma your parents have given to you over your childhood years is life-changing. You are suddenly free to love, to Love your parents for who they are, to love yourself for who you are. Free to move forward and be the awesome person you are meant to be, with a heart that is free to beat and a body that needs not hold onto any resentments.

*If you are triggered by your child:*

When our child behaves in a certain way – for example, they cry – we are sometimes triggered by it, usually because we are reacting in the way *our parents* treated us when we cried.

This is the section that many of our parents missed until it was too late, such as their children growing up and then triggering them because we have allowed them to trigger us – and of course the cycle goes on and on.

Let's explore the concept of crying a bit further. I shall make a broad statement here, only qualified by the thousands of conversations I have had with my peers over the years: this particular trigger – crying – has to be the biggest triggers known to my generation, Gen X.

Why? Because a lot of us were told not to cry or in fact, express any emotion. Not sure why? Ask your parents' parents. It's the family gift of triggers that keeps on giving, particularly to little boys, as this outburst of emotion was once largely seen as a sign of weakness. Thankfully we are not in that era anymore, and we appreciate that a bloody big cry actually releases cortisol from our body.

Cortisol is a by-product of stress, which of course is a by-product of having a hard time in life. When you cry, your body is eliminating the build up of cortisol, which over time, inhibits your immune system. It's biology at its most brilliant, but for whatever reason society deemed it inappropriate, and we started moving away from our natural states of being. It's OK; we now know what to do, and we cry we must when we need to let out stress. But the sheer sound of crying, especially for Gen X and older, is particularly affecting.

The minute you feel anything other than empathy when you hear your baby or child cry, then stop and identify what you are feeling. Once you identify this feeling, then know this: the reason you are feeling this emotion is because *this* is how you were dealt with when you were a child who cried. I can reassure you that once you identify this, the strong emotion that you are feeling dissipates – simply because you acknowledge that it is not yours, and belongs to your parents instead.

Once you have acknowledged this, say these words: "They are not me. I am not my parents." Say this with love and compassion.

Repeat this over and over again, until you have released yourself from the trigger of the past memory – and propelled yourself back into the present moment, ready to continue to feel the correct emotion for your child, such as empathy versus anger or fear.

Once you have released yourself from the trigger, and the child has stopped crying because you have attended to their needs, the next step is to come back into the present moment and connect with your child. And then, during the moments following the release of a trigger, it's important to relax and ground yourself as a parent.

**The Grounded Parent Meditation:**

The importance of grounding yourself as a person cannot be overstated, but as a parent its even more necessary.
Sleep deprivation and confusion with the new role you are taking on can lead to living in your head and scattering your energy fields.
Grounding yourself is an ancient activity that helps you reconnect and realign your energies on Earth.
When we allow our body to connect with the Earth we enhance our mental, physical and emotional wellbeing.
Let us Begin.

Sit up straight
Close your eyes
Slowly Take a breath and Inhale through your nose **(inhale)**
and Exhale through your mouth **(exhale)**
....and Relax.
**Feel** your **body** relax.
Again inhale through your Nose, **(inhale)**
Hold it.
And as you Exhale, **(exhale)**
Relax.
And one more Slow, steady breath through your nose. **(inhale)**

And as you exhale, **(inhale)**
Feel your body relax.

Place your feet firmly on the floor and really feel the floor underneath your feet.
Feel from your heels to your toes, every surface of floor your feet are touching.
Now imagine you have roots growing from your feet deep into Mother Earth.
Feel the roots getting deeper and deeper into the floor, grounding you right now, in your chair, where you are, as a Parent.
Feel roots Growing deep **deep** into the ground.
Through the floor, deep into the Earth, just like a Tree.

You are grounding yourself into Mother Earth.
Feel the roots going deeper and deeper into Mother Earth, connecting you with Earth and Anchoring you to feel safe, strong and grounded, right now, in your chair, where you are, as a Parent.
Your roots are strong, they are deep and they are stable.

You have now Grounded yourself as a Parent.
I want you now, to feel the chair under your legs.
As you move your awareness up your body, squeeze a muscle and move your joints to really ground yourself Deeper into the chair.
Deeper into the earth.
Feel your awareness move from your ankles, calves, knees.
Feel the chair under your thighs, buttocks, hips.
Sit down into the chair, FEEL your back into the chair.

Feel a deep sense of relaxation as you Inhale and Exhale out any stress and worries that might be on your mind.
Feel yourself breathing in a deep sense of connection with Mother Earth, and breathing out any stress or worry from your day, week, or month.

Feel the sensation in shoulders, give them a shrug up and down to deeply relax.
Feel your neck, chin and Jaw.
Place the tip of your tongue on the roof of your mouth.
This helps to relax your jaw.
Feel your nostrils relax, your nose, your eyelids and eyebrows.
Then all the way up to the energy at the top of your head.
Feel yourself from your head down to your toes.
Feel yourself grounding deeper and deeper into mother earth.

And just BE.. Let us breath into our body again.
Inhale through your nose   (**inhale**)
and Exhale through your mouth   (**exhale**)
Relax.
Breath in through your nose   (**inhale**)
and Exhale through your mouth   (**exhale**)
and Relax.
One more time, Breath in through your nose   (**inhale**)
and Exhale through your mouth   (**exhale**).
And Relax.  Deeply Relax.

Enjoy feeling yourself deeply in your body, present and empowered by your ability to ground yourself. Just Sit.

Just Be.

Remain seated for the rest of the music and let yourself Relax deep within the Present Moment connecting with yourself and Mother Earth.

**Step 4 - Tantrums**

Tantrums are a triggers best friend, both for the parent *and* the child.  And if you aren't prepared emotionally – in other words, you haven't got your "shit" together – the everyday tantrum can pull the rug out from under your feet.

Sometimes, when a tantrum occurs, you will be triggered by how you feel about the tantrum, so deal with that trigger as instructed above. But how do you deal with the tantrums if you *aren't* being triggered?

 Tantrums are an expression of anger, and anger is a derivative of fear.  So, look at why they are scared. (Don't freak out, their fear is not necessarily a deep, dark one – usually it is the fear of missing out, or the fear of losing their toy.).  Are they scared to go to the party because they are shy (fear of new people)? Are they upset about leaving because they were just watching their favourite TV show (fear of missing out)?  Once you figure out what they are scared of – and in some cases it's as easy as calming them, asking them what they are scared, fearful, of or concerned about,  and they will tell you – then you are able to reassure them with love.

Often during a tantrum, the child has reached a whereby all you can do for them is to hold space.

Do you remember moments whereby you just howled and howled and howled? Overwhelmed by life, falling apart can sometimes be the only way to truly get back together. Unable to communicate, we sometimes just want someone to hold our hand whilst we fall apart.

Children need to know we are there for them, and in the moments when they have been completely overwhelmed by a situation, a long howling may be the solution *they* need. If this triggers you, then deal with it, as per Step 3, and then just be as physically near to your child as they will let you, and lovingly hold space. Gently say you love them, and that they are safe and OK. This is oftentimes all they need, a space to release. Little people have *big* feelings, and quite often that is just what a tantrum is: a *big feeling*.

Kids often don't know what they are feeling, which is overwhelming, so they just let it out in an apparent tantrum. Hormone changes, perception changes, and milestones can be overwhelming, and even grown adults find it hard to cope – so imagine being a new human in today's world? It must be overwhelming, and who are we to assume they won't need a good long scream about it? It's important to ensure they remain safe, and of course feel loved, and I've often sat quietly in the room, murmuring quietly and calmly, "I love you," "it's OK," and "I'm here" whilst my child lay on the floor and just howled.

The pre-cursor to the long tears? Honestly, it can be as simple as giving the child juice instead of milk. It's just been a build up of misunderstandings for them, and then, BAM – a big feeling, and they are on the floor and mum and dad are left wondering, *WTF? Why the dramatic reaction?*

Really delving into Step 3 will ensure that you aren't triggered and are able to hold space for another human being – this takes practise. Mothers can physically react to their children's tears (as her child was once a part of her physical body), and quite often mothers talk about how much their body hurts when their child cries. Self-love and self-care help you to tolerate this physical pain.

Enjoying a moment of pure connection between a parent and child will help to stop a tantrum. Also, it helps to remember that you are alleviating *their* future tantrums and triggers when *they* become parents.

It's not enough to just feed, bathe, and bed them; nurture them with a mindful and respectful love. You are paying it forward by giving them emotional wealth. Imagine how incredible the world would be if we can raise un-triggered, emotionally stable human beings; I truly believe that this is the most important thing you can do for your child, the world, and yourself. Raise the future generations of this world to be sane, strong, independent, capable of loving freely, and emotionally intelligent, freeing them up to do great things for this beautiful planet and for the future of mankind.

I have faith and hope that we can make the world a better place by parenting well, and I will never stop rising daily to better myself , to raise my children with love, and to help others to do the same.

# Chapter 5.

## CONTINUE TO RISE

You've had your baby. You're breastfeeding. You've sorted out your pre-parenting shit and are stepping into your "truth" as a mother or father.

But maybe your birth went wrong. Perhaps you ended up with the C-section you had been dreading. You wondered if your fears had manifested this shit show, and you can't stop wondering if it was all your fault.

Or you had the perfect birth, and then baby was in need of medical attention, and you weren't able to have the early days skin -to-skin time with them. Of course, you blame yourself, or your partner, or the midwife – that woman stuffed up your perfect birth!

Whatever your journey, you can't help but feel it was messed up and you deserved better. In fact, you might even have nightmares about it still. Or – and this may come as some relief to mothers to realise this is "normal" to feel – you may even blame your baby for your imperfect birth. *How* dare *he get sick? If only he was around the right way! I wish he was healthy. Look what he put me through. And so on...*

It may still be a regular "thing" you discuss at your mother's group, and then you realise you start to become triggered by people who had the "perfect." birthing experience. Regular thoughts of *Screw them!* or *That's not fair!* may rage through your head. You may even jokingly tell someone to shut the front door about how amazing they had it – you may even be honest and cry on a friend's shoulder about your experience, even though by this stage your child is now three.

OK, so now lets' back up a LOT and do some work on clearing years of torment and storms *before* baby gets to three and *before* you're about to slap any mum who dared to have that calm home birth you longed for so much. Or let's try something different: let's think, *Well done, her*, take a deep breath, and then sort out our inner storm so that we can have inner peace and spread the love. We are, after all, all God's children!

I created this meditation after doing some intensive self-forgiveness work. I released the judgements I had on myself regarding the birth of my first baby not being as "natural" as I had wanted it to be, and then I released the anger I had at the midwife that I swore just hated my guts. I now feel nothing but acceptance and peace for both of my births – they were truly gifts, and perfect in their own ways. Just as your experience can be for you.

Inner peace with parenting is totally available – you just need to be available to do the work. After learning to forgive your birthing experience, you will feel a lot more at peace with your own journey.

There are many things you can do to enhance or "take back" your power ,in terms of what you have missed out on. Skin-to-skin cuddles with your toddler, for example, tummies are touching, are so powerful.

Oxytocin is released from skin-to-skin until the day you cease to be in human form, so please hold hands with your lover, keep cuddling your children, and never underestimate the power of a kiss on the cheek, for both the giver and the receiver.

**Birthing Forgiveness Mediation:**

This meditation may help you come to terms with the beginning of your Mothering Journey not being how you expected it to be.
A traumatic Birthing experience, no matter how big or small, can bring about Stress that can amplify even the simplest challenge in relation to your Journey as a Parent.
Acknowledging this now is important and can help remove resentment or grief.
Let us do the work, face our traumas and move through our fears, so as to be able to enjoy our journey as a parent.
Let us begin.

Sit up straight
Close your eyes,
Slowly Take a breath and Inhale through your nose **(inhale)**
and Exhale through your mouth **(exhale)**
....and Relax.
Feel your body relax.
Again inhale through your Nose, **(inhale)**
Hold it.
And as you Exhale, **(exhale)**
Relax.

And one more Slow, steady breath through your nose. **(inhale)**
And as you exhale, **(exhale)**
Feel your body relax.

And now, become aware of your Birthing experience.
Visualise where you were, and the people you were with.
Become fully conscious of the situation you experienced and allow any Emotions surrounding the Birth to come to the surface..
What is this making you feel right now?
It's ok, you are safe.

Take note of the Emotions you are feeling.
Allow them to rise to the surface, no matter how strong they are.
It's ok, you are safe.

Now Accept the way you are feeling.
You have rights to feel anger, to be afraid, to have strong beliefs and anxious limitations.
Your feelings **never** need justification.
Sit now amongst these feelings, and breath.
It's ok, you are safe.

Now we face the people responsible for your pain.
I want you to stand in front of All the other people involved in your Birthing experience.
The Doctor, the Nurses, Your partner, the Midwives, even your baby.
Now tell them how you feel. Tell them everything.
Tell them you were hurting.
Tell them you felt angry at them.
Really tell them what you felt at your baby's birth right now.

(pause)

Now You will only be able to let go and get on with your life once you've accepted these other people.
To do this, you now have to put yourself in their shoes.
Can you see things from their perspective.
Were they doing the best they could at the time?
Were their actions simply a reflection of them doing the best they could?
Visualise this now and try to better Understand their Intentions.
(pause)
Have you been able to Understand this?
If not, that's fine, this might take time,
If so, then this is where you will be able to accept them and Let GO.
For all the other people involved in the Birth.
For the staff, for your Partner, but Most importantly, For YOURSELF.

Now....to let go what you feel for them.
You have to forgive yourself.

And you do have to let Go.
Breath in (**inhale**)
Then exhale and Let Go.
Just, Let, Go.

Say out loud,
I Forgive Others
I Forgive my Baby
I Forgive Myself
Say this again.
I forgive myself.
(pause)

How do you feel?
Release it all. (**exhale**)
Its OK, you are safe.

Now, Feel empowered by the courage you have shown for yourself.
You have faced your past, and that's simply amazing.
You have the power of your mind to bring forth new Love and Identity.
Continue to do this exercise until you have reached a place of complete acceptance. Regarding everyone involved with your birthing experience....including forgiving your beautiful self.

You are doing the best you can.
You are doing a Wonderful Job.

Please remember that Self Love and Letting Go with Forgiveness takes practice.
Learn to Mother with Love and Mother with Courage and Joy.
Continue to listen to this as many times as you need.
Be Kind to yourself in your Journey as Mother.

This can be done by partners, too (remember, empowering our partners to rise into their roles is unconditional love).

It is tumultuous times in this day and age, and inner storms are aplenty. We are so overstimulated, – all of us! Technology is a blessing and curse, and this is important information to learn: our children's neurons are overstimulated by watching TV, iPads, phones, screens etc. What happens is this – their brains fire off all of the activity that replicates what they are watching, but because their bodies are stationary, it creates an imbalance in their systems.

So, the solution to this is that when they put down the technology, we should allow their bodies to burn off all the energy that's been played out in their brains – this goes for us, too!

The best way to create balance is to do some intensive physical activity straight after a session on technology. For the kids, maybe a jump on the trampoline? A bike ride? For the adults...hey, why not the same? Unless, of course, you feel like you're going to wee yourself or your insides are going to end up on the trampoline mat (which is what it feels like for me, thanks prolapse).

Either way, exercising our bodies to catch up with the overactive neurons is the key to balance here. But sometimes we are trying to multitask before the kids get to bed, and before you know it something snappy was said and you may have been a crabby bitch to one (or all) of them. If you let that stuff go, and continue to scream and yell at your kids, a lot of resentment from all parties is going to escalate. Although I promise you, the kids will get over it quicker than you – until they are adults and then need therapy because you were a crazy-arse-bitch-face who never bothered to get her shit together and who kept cramming wine in her face to deal with the overstimulating prick of an environment you are all in! But LOL, that so won't happen right? Because we are here, fixing that.

Children are resilient, and unless you're beating them (which if you are, stop doing that and get help NOW), a screaming match here and there is forgivable and curable. Also, the power of an apology can never be underestimated – are YOU modelling good behaviour by admitting to your children that you were wrong?

As long as you realise it cannot continue, and you promise to get your stuff together, then here is a meditation to help you forgive yourself:

## I Forgive Myself Meditation:

This meditation is created to help you forgive yourself if your emotions have sent you outside the window of tolerance and you have lost your temper at your child. Regardless of how old your child is and the circumstances involved, the Parent guilt monster can send us into a depression if we get too hard on ourselves.

Losing your temper with a child is never ideal, but we must acknowledge that we are often pushed to our limits due to exhaustion, sleep deprivation and emotional triggers.

The focus immediately following a flare up is on the repair of the relationship with your child, you do this by reassuring them that you still love them and perhaps take some deep breaths together.

This meditation is best done once the child is calm, and you are in need of forgiving yourself.

So Let us Begin.

## Music starts....

Sit up straight
Eyes closed
Slowly Take a breath and Inhale **(inhale)**
and Exhale **(exhale)**
....and Relax.
Feel your body relax.
Again inhale through your Nose, **(inhale)**

Hold it.
And as you Exhale, **(exhale)**
Relax.
And one more Slow, steady breath through your nose. **(inhale)**
And as you exhale, **(exhale)**
Feel your body relax.

Bring yourself into the present moment by deliberately asking yourself,
What is my experience right now,
In thoughts, Feelings and Bodily sensations?
(pause)
Then gently redirect your full attention to breathing,
to each in breath
and to each out breath as they follow.
one after the other.

Emotion regulation depends on our ability to be mindful
of the fluctuations in our level of body sensations.
We can learn to recognize when we are in our danger zone,
and bring ourselves back to safety through grounding skills.

By Turning your full attention to your breathing,
This can help to remind you to notice when you are heading into rough waters
and then help to steer you back on course.

Try not to be your own worst critic.
Forgive your slip ups, it is OK to be human and to react.
The magic, is in the repair.

The repair is in reassuring your child that you still love them.

Right now, I want you to let go of the angry situation with your child.
I want you to take a deep breath in (**inhale**)
and as you exhale (**exhale**)
I want you to release the guilt.
Just let it go.

Three more times.

Take a long deep breath in through your nose (**inhale**)
and as you exhale (**exhale**)
Release the guilt.

breath in through your nose (**inhale**)
and as you exhale (**exhale**)
release the guilt.
Just let it go.

One more long deep breath in through your nose (**inhale**)
and as you exhale (**exhale**)
I want you to release it all, just relax.


Now say to yourself,
I forgive me
I am only human
The magic is in the repair

I forgive me
I am only human
The magic is in the repair.

Losing your temper doesn't make you a monster.
It makes you human and that is what you are.

Letting go of your guilt and moving forward with love
will heal all mistakes
Focus on keeping yourself grounded daily
This will help you keep your cool
And Free you to do what you do best
and that is Love and Nurture your child.

Be kind to yourself in your journey as a mother or father.

*Chapter 6.*

# GO FORTH AND CONQUER

When I am putting my babies (not quite so little any more) to sleep, I place my finger into their sleepy hand, that even at 6 and 10 still rest quite remarkably as they did when they were first born. Palms facing upwards, fingers curled in, my finger or thumb fitting nicely in the curved space.

I then gaze at their sleeping angel faces with overwhelming love and gratitude...then I always whisper, "Thank you, thank you for choosing me to be your mum".

Then I thank God, because it is through having children that I know He exists.

How can he not? There is no way that a love so perfect and pure exists without a Magnificent and Powerful Being. If you don't believe in God, that's fine, however for me, I simply know that these children could not have been placed so perfectly in my arms any other way.

I never go a day when I am with them that I am not breath-taken by how much love they have elicited from me. How much joy they bring to me, simply by existing.

I am also inspired, driven even, by the need to rise every single day and absolutely "show up" for them, for me and for life.

The honour it is for me to become a Mother doesn't come at a price, it comes with a responsibility that I have truly and honestly cherished from the minute I conceived my Emily (the beginning of my rise) and then David (the completion).

From that very first moment I promised Emily to "get my shit together", I have woken up every day energised to do better.  Focused on being always better, stronger, more capable, prettier, cleaner, smarter, more qualified, healthier, more and more and better and better.  I don't always "feel" better, stronger or smarter, in fact, it is those moments of face down on the floor, or hiding out the front of the house crying because I can't deal with not one but two tantrums at the same time, that have been the moments to "make me".

I realised once I became a Mother that my struggles were my strengths.

I simply learnt to thrive after a challenge, and all because I wanted to be the best Mum I could possible be.

I apologise for my meltdowns, I cry openly with my children and I am sometimes so lazy I eat chocolate for months on end and wonder why the kids and I are buzzing at all hours of the evening.

But I never miss a night time story, I never EVER miss a "baby mine" lullaby (we have a promise in my home, no matter how tired mummy is, no matter how late it is, or how out of control the night time routine gets - my children ALWAYS get that lullaby "baby mine" from Dumbo) and if that is the only opportunity I got that day to rise for my children, then I bloody made it.

In all honesty I have not stopped, nor will I ever stop, picking myself up, dusting myself off, throwing the blocks of chocolate and ciggies in the bin (oh yes, that old chestnut addiction still on my back, that's ok, I haven't touched a drink for nearly 4 years Amen) and starting my "rise" every single day with every single breath I have.

Does it sound exhausting? No way, it's exhilarating. Motherhood is the best gift Life (God) has ever given me and my two children are incredible teachers, mentors and friends. But mostly, they are just incredible children.

Being a Mother is an opportunity to start again.

To Rise into the person you always knew you wanted to be.

To Rise and Rise to raise the future generations of the world.

It is, quite simply, the most important job in the world.

It is my favourite job (and I have had plenty I assure you, well over 100) and I cherish every moment, even the stressed and shit ones. Because they are usually the ones I grow from, however, the cards of "I love you Mummy" plastered over the fridge, in my wallet and cuddles and kisses every single morning and night are also ones I grow from too.

If you are struggling as a Mother, I urge you to stop, drop and just love your child.

If you need help shaking off addiction, bad habits, better health, leaving a toxic relationship, always, I mean always, put the safety love and respect of those children first and foremost.

If there is every any doubt in your mind on what to do, just think what is the right solution for the child, putting them first is paramount in making the right decision every single time.

It may change the trajectory of your life, it may feel scary, but I assure you, the love you have for your child will give you the courage and strength you need.

If you can, work on yourself and I mean, work. Don't stop until you are looking into the mirror and not just liking what you see, but Loving Her!!

Do EVERYTHING this world has to offer, get on your knees and pray, repent and give your life to Jesus, do sound healings, art therapy, counselling, psychology, group therapy, sister circles, nature walks, dance therapy, meditation retreats, talk to your best friend, go to church, volunteer somewhere, journal out the bad thoughts, breath work, cold water therapy and exercise that trauma out of the cells in your body...there are books to read (yes including the bible!), clips to watch and oh so many wonderful practitioners out there that will blow your mind on health and wellbeing...explore every corner of the world, find your tribe, seek your soul and DON'T STOP SEARCHING TIL YOU FIND HER.

This is ALL YOU HAVE TO DO TO RISE as a Mother.

It is ALL your children need you to do.

Don't worry about the housework, worry about your INNER work.

Worry about your psychology, worry about not having to worry about whether or not you are going to have anxiety going to a party or supermarket or cleaning up a poo explosion in the middle of the highway....when you become WHOLE and LOVE yourself...the face down moments are moments to cherish JUST AS MUCH as the first time they say "I love you Mummy".

Never ever stop trying or working or achieving getting your Rise, even if it's just remembering to put clean knickers on today. Tomorrow you do clean socks as well...and you keep rising until your whole body is clean, then your mind, then your beautiful fresh and fearless SOUL.

When you are whole and RISE for your children, you are **completely** and **absolutely** empowered to be raising the future generation.

So as I send you off, hopefully encouraging you to do everything you possibly can do to be the utmost best mother you can, I leave you with this.

Loving our children with everything we have and can and should and will; is the most important thing you can every truly do. Focus on Love and Love will Focus on you.

God Bless and Love them with all your might.

Shona xoxox

# RESOURCES TO RISE

https://www.breastfeeding.asn.au

https://www.llli.org

https://www.breastfeedingnetwork.org.uk

http://www.canadianbreastfeedingfoundation.org

https://breastfeeding.support/directory/

https://www.lcanz.org/find-a-lactation-consultant/

If you cannot find an IBCLC to help you on your journey – you can book a consult with me here: riseofthemother@gmail.com

If you want to support your nutrition, like I did with JuicePlus, you can consult with me here: riseofthemother@gmail.com

If you are interested in running your own business so you can stay at home with your baby, then contact me here: riseofthemother@gmail.com

Find me on Instagram:
https://www.instagram.com/savingtheworldoneboobatatime/

# Meditations

https://www.patreon.com/riseofthemother

The Let Down Meditation, P58

The Expressing Let Down Meditation, P60

Inner Child Meditation, P67

Parent Cleanse Meditation, P70

The Mother Identity Meditation, P76

The Father Identity Meditation, P.79

The Grounded Parent Meditation, P.84

Birthing Forgiveness Mediation, P.90

I Forgive Myself Meditation, P.94

# About the Author

Shona Reidy lives in Victoria, Australia and is a mother to two beautiful children. She enjoys breath work, meditation, bike rides and long walks on the beach. For Shona, life is busy as a single parent and nothing has ever beaten the feeling she has when witnessing her children grow and walk their own paths as strong and creative human beings. Her daughter was the beginning of her incredible journey, and her son is the perfect completion of her experience in motherhood.

Through journeying extensively herself, Shona has dedicated the last twelve years to helping other mothers rise and walk their own journeys to become the best mothers they can be. Her hope is that the role of mother becomes a more valued one in society, and is recognized monetarily so that mothers don›t have to "leave" their babies to earn money.